INFINITE
THREADS

100 Indigenous Insights from Old Maori Manuscripts

MARIKO B. RYAN

Mariko B. Ryan
www.marikobryan.nz

Printed in Aotearoa / New Zealand
First Printing 2020
First Edition 2020

ISBN: 978-0-473-52614-6

10 9 8 7 6 5 4 3 2 1

Edited by: Nancy Pile, ZooWrite
Cover design: R. Kamira (Te Rarawa), Aotearoa (New Zealand)
Tiki image: Tanetiki Morgan (Te Rarawa), Aotearoa (New Zealand)

DEDICATION

There can only be one dedication. To the man with the foreknowledge and prudence to leave this precious legacy. We never met in our physical lives, as we walk this place in different times. So, I leave you with the words of my kaumatua, elder, Joe Cooper, who as a seventeen-year-old, recounted his memories of my great-grandfather with great awe:

> "Takou was a tall, striking, and noble Rangatira, an Ariki in his own right. He was a Seer, a Matakite, with ancestral historical foresight and eloquence. He articulated te reo with finesse, gesturing his tokotoko up high when ritualising karakia, celestial and ethereal. He was leader of the Rangatira Elders, known in Hokianga as the Wananga. One cannot miss the swinging gold chain of his pocket watch within the long overcoat."

Kaumatua: Esteemed Elder
Rangatira: An esteemed chief, leader with qualities of nobility
Ariki: A paramount chief or leader with a concern for the integrity and prosperity of the people
Matakite: A visionary, prophet, seer
Te Reo: The Maori language

Tokotoko: Ritualistic walking or oratory stick or staff, some say a conduit for connection to Atua (the Deities)

Karakia: Invocation

Hokianga: Region including a harbour situated in the far north of Aotearoa (New Zealand)

Wananga: A traditional school of esoteric and higher learning. The esoteric knowledge sessions

From a handwritten note given to the author 27 March 2010 by Joe Cooper (Panguru, Hokianga), previous Chair of Kahui Kaumatua (of Te Runanga o Te Rarawa) and Te Runanga o Te Rarawa Historical Treaty Claims Settlement Negotiator. Uncle Joe is the son of Dame Whina Cooper, a Maori leader who organised her first protest action at just 18, and led the Maori Land March in her eighties. Her activism helped forge the start of a new, albeit still testing, relationship with the Crown. She was a peer of The Old Man, the Sage.

MEANING OF THE TIKI

The tiki was created by artist Tanetiki Morgan (Te Rarawa). A tiki often represents an ancestor who is no longer with us. In this case, he represents the author's great-grandfather—the tohunga, sage—who wrote the manuscripts that are the inspiration for this book. He is also the great, great-grandfather of the artist. The tiki holds a quill because he is the writer of old knowledge. He features the split tongue because he is an orator of esoteric knowledge, spoken in the language of our people; and he also speaks the secret language of Atua, the deities.

Table of Contents

Nitty-Gritty

Chapter One
Outlandish Territory

THERE ARE TIMES OF WHICH WE SHALL NEVER SEE THE LIKE OF AGAIN. The world has veered into some outlandish territory where the sun bleeds red and the moon slumps in the sky and we overrun the planet, leaving footprints everywhere. We strip the earth of dignity for an imagined concept called civilisation. We strip ourselves of dignity for an imagined concept called freedom. We lurch from one episode to the next in pursuit of purpose or pleasure or liberty. Many of us live where the right to hate surpasses the right to love. And we depend on governments, corporations, and institutions for moral and spiritual leadership they do not possess.

Too many leaders exude confidence and power, but are bullies, liars, and bigots. Truth rarely comes out of the mouths of those whose incessant rants and bared teeth fill the silence. Yet, they are urged on by followers who shove megaphones into their clammy hands. Amplified voices assure us there is much to fear, shadows everywhere, we deserve more, and they will keep us safe. We wait and wait. All the while, we make them richer. They make us stupider. The insane appear to be leading the insane. And it is folly.

Oh, the fatalist will say there is nothing we can do. They will be right if enough of us choose it. You, dear reader, appear to know this. To see truth we need to keep our eyes open even when the view is appalling. To keep them shut invites the demolition of ourselves and each other. There is no other outcome. But changing people's views must surely be one of the more difficult endeavours. All sides believe their righteousness. No force or logic or plea will change an entrenched mind and closed eyes. Whoever discovers what will, will surely change the course of history forever.

Chapter Two
You Don't Have To Clap

MAORI, A COLONIALIST, A MISSIONARY, A SCHOLAR AND A *MOKO-KAKARIKI*—ALL WALKED INTO A BAR ... because no great story starts with someone drinking a *spicy chai latte with black tea and cinnamon*. A group of rivals in a friendly establishment telling a few tentative yarns before getting to the truth could be the perfect way to diffuse tension before the real *korero*, discussion, begins. True, the story doesn't start well. But, I declare, if they do not leave with their arms around each other by the close of the evening, then we are in trouble. I would like to think that after their stories are retold and resolved, they will each know inherently that none is singularly perfect, and that in reviewing their part from the perspective of another, they will recognise their *whanaungatanga*—kinship. I hope they will come to the firm conclusion that the only thing worth pursuing is reconciliation and restitution, and they need to work together if they are to avoid the edge of the same cliff.

And what about us? We hitch our identities to our stories. They tell us who we are and who we belong to. If someone distorts our version, we don't like it. But of course, it is their story to tell, and even they endeavour to tell it as truthfully as they can. Still, we have, until recent times, been presented mostly with the victors' versions of history, reinforced by schooling and popularly integrated into our perception of facts. The shelves of old libraries are full of these creaking truths. Nowadays, the defeated sometimes get to write history too. Even when lives, land and knowledge have been disrupted, the stories often remain. Telling them is how we move as a collective towards recovery after loss. It is how we restore wisdom and pride. It is what we do after the initial pain has receded—when there is room for the weary mind to share the story wider. This book is one of them.

This story may be different to those some of us have grown up with. Or it may be so familiar that some of us feel like we have come home. I will tell it from the perspective of some of my old people, of me and mine. Not always beautiful. Not always palatable. We may cower when the curtain hiding the harsh truths is yanked open—especially if it invokes something uncomfortable, something we don't like repeated. We may prefer it be sanitised. We may prefer to change the subject, accuse the storyteller of not 'getting over it' and we'd rather forget it.

Let us deal with this matter.

Our discomfort serves only us. I have learnt it holds no value for the storyteller and it doesn't change the story. Let us not behave like consumers, only gleaning what is agreeable. Let us check ourselves. Knowledge is not a right. It is a gift. Some have fought hard to keep or retrieve it.

We may have to consider that we are not the primary recipients because the first beneficiaries of knowledge should be those from whom it is sourced. Sharing it first within this group is part of the healing process. During this time, we may only be a witness. After, when the source group is satisfied they are in charge of their own stories, they may extend the audience. Not being a consumer means understanding this is not a transaction, but a privilege.

This is me telling my story to you, dear reader. You are my extended audience. For a time, I have your mind and maybe your heart, and I'm keen to honour that. In the end, you will decide its value. If I may borrow the words of a lovely old codger friend, now passed, who used to say, *'You don't have to clap if you don't like it'.*

MARIKO B. RYAN

Chapter Three
Trajectory

I T IS A REGRETTABLE IRONY THAT WE USE THE WORD 'MAORI' TO DESCRIBE OURSELVES. The coloniser appropriated it to render some kind of catch-all distinction between themselves and the natives. It was an 'othering'. A convenience that stuck and a term occasionally used with derogatory intent, even today. Back then our people used the word to denote something as being normal, the default. In any case, I use the word sparingly and only to give you, dear reader, a point on the horizon.

So, my *tangata whenua*, people of the land, indigenous, native, first nations, Maori (as in 'normal') great-grandfather was born in the last quarter of the 1800s. It was when the great yellow fog crept through the poorest districts of London, dragging the weak along with it. The children sang and sang. They were nursery rhymes alluding to devastation, horror, pretty dresses, and little neckties. Still the fog came. Again, and again. It was when, under anxious skies, invaders crept to newly surveyed boundaries to observe the people of Parihaka from a distance as they peacefully ploughed and fenced. The children sang and sang. They sang for peace. They sang to keep their lands. Still, the 1,500-strong constabulary marched in. Dirt. Blood. Tears. It was when, in the reflecting light of the Hokianga, The Old Man's tribal homelands were stripped. Tree by tree by tree. Erosion and trading ships came—one with the other. And the children sang of kinship, love and hope. Still, the native forests of the Great Immortal *Tane-Mahuta* sailed over the bar to Australia. Cows munched newly grassed paddocks while busting wind into unspoiled skies. And the burial grounds were defiled forever more.

Colonisation changed the way The Old Man's generation lived, worked, and practised their beliefs. What it provided—economic opportunity—could so easily be withdrawn. The dependency on government policies and services, and introduced religion and education set the next generation up for unemployment, poverty, and the fateful abandonment of their land. Sure enough, in the 1950s the government abruptly shut down the dairy factory, and overnight the farms were no longer viable. The people left in droves to find work. Several lost their land to the cogs and wheels of bureaucratic skulduggery.

The brutal passage of colonisation is harsh and unforgiving. Even when the war is over, it's not really over. That generation was besieged with racism, beatings, and all manner of abuse at the hands of the colonialists and their agents. The goal was to belt the noble savage into submission. My father rarely spoke of it, but when he did, he refused to offer detail. Instead, he clung to his rage, sharing it regularly throughout our growing-up years and letting it consume him into his old age.

He, like many of his elders, tried to direct his children towards what he hoped was a better life—a Western way of living. Where opportunity beckoned. Where it would be safe.

It was a façade. Our people would never truly be assimilated nor reap the privileges of our white cousins. At best, it would take multiple inter-generational shifts and a step change away from well-embedded institutionalised racism. Unable to confront the elusive and untouchable perpetrators, some of our people turned on themselves. Heart-breaking and avoidable tragedies, and cyclical behaviours were normalised. Of this, I will say little. The story is a universal one experienced by colonised peoples around the world. It does not need to be repeated here because there are plenty to tell it, and you and I have important business to attend to. However, many of our people were wrenched from a unique worldview that may have solidified their sense of identity and expectations and made a difference to the trajectory they took.

MARIKO B. RYAN

Chapter Four
Bobbing Beer Bottles

Many years ago, my once very good-looking and later beer-bellied welder father was partial to having a Pakeha—that is, 'of English descent'—wife. My once very sporty and later not-so-active but still petite clerk mother was partial to inheriting a sizeable Maori family. After they got together, his family refused to sanction his marriage to a white, non-Catholic woman. So, they sent cash and urged him to return to his tribal lands, back into the embrace of his relations.

After the welder and the clerk got together, she presented herself heavily pregnant to landlords while he stayed out of sight. They eventually secured a government Maori Affairs house in Auckland—the one my siblings and I grew up in.

A melting pot neighbourhood, it was the coffee-coloured people. The state houses around us were occupied by immigrant parents from several South Pacific Island nations and their New Zealand-born children. We were all vaguely related through historic ocean migrations evidenced by an expansive genealogy of dubious exactness. Yellow and orange and lime island-style shirts, bold flower lava-lavas, and joyful uninhibited song and laughter resounded between the blue, yellow, and green peeling-paint houses. The colour spectrum in an otherwise very beige suburb.

We were supplied with prefab schools with jungle gyms, and seagulls that flew over the playgrounds, so they could drop their slimy missiles on our heads. There were little plain churches made from concrete bricks, displaying nondescript wooden crosses. Cluttered corner dairies traded milk, butter, Sunday loaves and one-cent bubble gums. And there was an over-supply of rugby fields.

Our one pair of shoes was passed down from bigger feet to smaller feet until eventually somebody's toes wore holes through the leather. Winter flooding saw us tuck our skirt uniforms into our pants and lift our bags above the waterline. We'd wade out of the house and weave around bobbing empty beer bottles recently liberated by the rising waters from my father's crates and now stealthily floating out to the street to their emancipation. We'd slosh to school hoping the eels were still nibbling worms in the creek somewhere under swollen waters and not searching for a delicious pair of human legs.

After the waters receded, we'd return to find our chain-link fence decorated length and breadth with used toilet paper and raw sewage hanging prettily off the wire. I thought it rather intriguing. My father didn't.

We holidayed at a beach campground in a big green canvas tent with flapping sides. Our grandmother would make delicious fry-bread on a gas stove under a pine tree.

Enough to feed all the kids in the camp until every single one could point to their protruding belly button—*ka puta te pito*—indicating they were full. She'd mix, knead, and fry for hours, and send my father out to buy more flour rather than have one child still hungry.

MARIKO B. RYAN

Chapter Five
The Old Man

One fortuitous day and quite by accident, I became acquainted with my great-grandfather. I have an inherited personality trait—curiosity with a touch of obsession and a love of old things. It saw me wander into our country's most eminent colonial museum, where he unexpectedly came to my attention. Long story short, eventually I came to be a *kaitiaki*, a guardian of his manuscripts, faced with a decision about what to do with them. I promise to tell that story in the next book, but for now, let me introduce him. You will meet him in these pages. He is The Old Man and sometimes the Ancestor or the Sage. Towering and straight of posture and in possession of an Orator's walking stick. My elders say he was a leader who served his community and an exponent of tribal lore who led the old knowledge sessions. He had been taught by the old Sages before him. They also disclosed, some with hesitancy, that he was a seer and a shapeshifter in the form of a *moko-kakariki*—the emerald green gecko.

The Old Man spent his life preserving his people's oral traditions, writing into carefully guarded manuscripts for over 50 years. It required an exceptional amount of personal determination and focus. Access to writing materials was limited to discarded books, some still possessing a portion of pages even if only barely attached to their stitch-binding. They were sourced from the church or some other colonial establishment. Later, he procured his grandchildren's exercise books, courtesy of the missionary-run native schools. My father and uncles, most likely, had to replenish their supplies regularly. Oh, how fortunate his great-granddaughter is to be in a position to purchase brand-new leather-bound books, and an array of colourful pens and pencils perfectly designed to inspire the writing process.

The Old Man's early writings showed a bright young fellow excited about his future and grappling with his identity and beliefs. The writings matured as he began to deal with the task of creating meticulous records. The words were in his native language, old, classical, beautiful to the ear. A free-flowing script, the style of an intelligent man, word art on the yellowed leaves of those discarded books. If only the pages had captured his voice too as he read what he had written out loud in the dim candlelight. He wrote and wrote until decades later the bite of an oncoming winter and his trembling hand revealed the dusky light of old age. By then, he had what was arguably the largest unpublished collection of its type by a single writer—historical accounts, ancient songs and chants, invocations, genealogies, and musings.

In 1953, the *Northern Times* described The Old Man as a 'Rangatira, a significant leader of his people', saying his death was 'the passing of one of the living storehouses of ancient lore'.

Yes, he wrote. Prolifically. Thousands upon thousands of pages.

It appears I have inherited his fondness for writing.

INFINITE THREADS

Chapter Six

Colonial Dreams

NOW SEEMS A PERFECT TIME TO TRANSITION TO THE INSIGHTS, AND YOUR CURIOSITY MUST BE DRIVING YOU TO MADNESS. Here we are, still lingering in the 1950s, and we must forge ahead, so we can arrive to the present time. And get down to the gritty business. Except, I haven't yet told you about the catalyst that prompted The Old Man to write so obsessively. And you'll most certainly need to know *why*.

So, come. Follow me back to the early 1800s—long before he was born. It was when the colonialists first arrived from Europe. They had a set mind to extend their empire-building aspirations to this cluster of islands deep in the South Pacific. Why would they not? It was over 100,000 square miles of enormous possibility— productive land and an abundance of tradable natural resources. And it was indisputably beautiful. Its geographic isolation from the rest of the world had produced a distinct biodiversity, flora and fauna. A scientist's playground. The climate was a temperate sub-tropical and sub-alpine wonderland. Tectonic uplifts and volcanic eruptions formed utterly majestic landscapes. Sharp snow-covered mountain peaks pierced wide incredibly blue skies. Pristine streams hurried through lush prehistoric forests and poured into oceans brimming with seafood. The roaring breakers of the West Coast answered the calmer, rolling waves of the East. The air was an irresistible, salty perfection. Every breath-taking part of this land called to the new immigrants to imagine new lives, possibilities, and futures. And the natives? Well, they could be dealt with. There was no perceived ethical barrier to the highly experienced colonial strategist.

They were tumultuous times for our people. Their ragged world was upended. However, they were resourceful. They quickly engaged the foreigners in equal measures of trade and skirmishes. But from 1840, the colonialists began installing the instruments of permanent political and economic governance, using a combination of convoluted administrative procedures and military might. Our people repeatedly stifled their attempts to accelerate land and resource acquisition by force or otherwise. The colonialists weren't well prepared for the resistance. They lacked the cultural maturity to engage with people who were equally, if not more so, astute strategists and warriors, armed with a strikingly different worldview. The colonialists soon realised despite their muskets and other modern weaponry they'd underestimated the ability of the natives to meet them in warfare. Maori warriors repeatedly brought British troops to a standstill. As a result, some semblance of cooperation was established here and there—it never lasted. The colonialists were determined to acquire the authority and resources they dreamt of.

So, on the brink of an internationally embarrassing failure, they regrouped and augmented their military resources with a temporary navy, complete with several riverboats, armoured barges, coastal boats, and a naval dockyard. Shiploads and shiploads of foreign soldiers spilled onto the beaches. Soon after, it was done.

MARIKO B. RYAN

Chapter Seven
River Of Myths

While the colonialists had won political and economic governance, they had yet to win the last bastion of colonial victory. Ideology. To do that, they needed to silence the sages. Until then, the method to transfer traditional expert knowledge comprised a rigorous oral transmission system demanding painstaking accuracy. It entailed the careful selection of future knowledge-keepers—the *tohunga*, the sages. The system was effective. Spiritual, medicinal, navigational, astronomical, agricultural, seasonal, and other knowledge was passed successfully from generation to generation. To succeed, the colonials needed to dismantle this system and thoroughly extinguish and replace the knowledge with their own. Their nominated battlegrounds were churches, classrooms, and courtrooms.

First, scholars and missionaries set about learning the native language and documenting the traditions and histories. They were somewhat untrained in matters of information gathering, methodology, and research, and were unfamiliar with the nuances of such a starkly different way of understanding the world. Many fancied themselves as favoured amongst the natives and believed they were privy to 'secret' information—with no clue as to whether they were being told fibs or not.

Some coloniser scholars were determined career-builders who sought to be recognised internationally. Their writings revealed their desire to control our people's narratives. As long as they endorsed each other's work and hushed any challenges, particularly from Maori scholars, they would have an uncontested opportunity to benefit from this new body of knowledge. By the turn of the century, they'd latched onto the magical 'hook' that would bring the international attention they sought.

The concept of Maori as *noble savages*—inhabitants of a paradise not corrupted by decadent civilisation—was bolstered by the sudden appearance of a monotheistic belief system in the writings of a Maori scribe who had converted to Christianity—and who was commissioned and directed to write. The coloniser scholars considered a single patriarchal-god belief system a key characteristic of a relatively civilised society. It was deemed superior to a polytheistic belief system with multiple deities who were often environmentally based and included female deities. The feminine aspects of spirituality in the colonisers' own belief systems had already been suppressed and discredited centuries beforehand—for example, they had already cast what my people might have called female sages as evil witches to be feared and burned.

In the absence of any corroborating evidence, the coloniser scholars scrambled for any shreds of proof they could gather—or invent—to reconceive our Maori belief system into a patriarchal and monotheistic one. They created a backstory to frame the new revelation, that, in fact, there was a single supreme god in Maori spiritualism, claiming it was a recently exposed secret that only the highest order of sages was privy to. Further, they claimed that any sage who didn't already know of this supreme god (which, it turns out, was all of the sages at the time) must, therefore, be of a lower order. It was claimed this god, whose name, it was said, should never be uttered, was so secret that revealing it would result in the most terrible of deaths. Further, revealing it to an outsider would result in even more severe punishment that could be visited upon generations. To tell would have required enormous courage—but apparently that courage was found. All was revealed by a Maori scribe in great detail to the coloniser scholars, one of whom, in turn, confessed the ease at which he could manipulate Maori scribes to write what he wanted. Another of his peers divulged he'd creatively filled gaps with information from elsewhere or had made it up. These admissions spoke to the idea that the dissemination of inauthentic information was a discretion that academia was comfortable with. This is surely enough to erode our confidence. But it doesn't end there.

The first Maori scholar to challenge these materials attracted the jagged edge of academic wrath. He was publicly berated for daring to tell them they had it wrong. Some years later, a new generation of Maori scholars also challenged the materials, but by then the idea of a supreme god had taken hold. An academic requirement to reference existing publications—a self-validating system still used today by universities—and the paucity of alternative materials left scholars with little choice but to draw from pro-monotheist research.

The decades that followed saw an eagerness by Maori scholars and their alignment with coloniser religious systems of belief were now commonplace. By now there were few scholars, Maori or otherwise, interested in dismantling the fiction. For a Maori scholar to dispute it was akin to admitting their ancestral sages were not of the coveted 'highest order', and that perhaps our people might not be noble after all. By the end of the 20th century, academic scrutiny and investigation into the origins of a supreme god appeared to be discretionary. Most scholars were simply regurgitating. The result is we are severely divided. Hook. Line. Sinker.

What of the missionaries? In the earlier years, they easily aligned the monotheist claim with conversion. It was a simple transition from a one-god belief system to another. It was not hard for our people to choose religion over the old beliefs. There were advantages. One of which was getting rid of the inconsistencies around how traditional beliefs were being applied in favour of a religion that included an instructional manual and a tour guide, and importantly, forgiveness. Men with prominent religious positions—bishops and priests—including our people, insisted they had sufficient expert training in traditional esoteric knowledge from the highest order of sages to confirm that a single supreme god existed before the white man came.

The obvious conflict of interest was rationalised and the momentum behind the claims strengthened.

Soon, a river of myths flowed into the beliefs and processes conducted by our people. Many of our own scholars invested their reputations in this river. Today, inconsistencies, confusion, and debate dominate our traditional practices. However, underneath, a bubbling spring, a challenge, is beginning to surface again. A new generation of Maori academics are now publishing their findings and challenging the older works. In part, this has been enabled by the recent changes to the access rules that apply to unpublished manuscripts in libraries and museums. A more thorough analysis of the sources indicates some of the original commissioned work is unreliable, falsification, and that some of it was misleadingly attributed to *tohunga*, sages.

Still, to question the controversial materials today attracts enthusiastic protestations. Many are convinced their information comes solely from their ancestors—passed down with meticulous precision—and is as reliable as the traditional oral methodologies used by the old sages two centuries ago. Some say that despite the questionable evidence, they emphatically 'know' one god to be true. Others don't care enough to investigate. We slip further and further away.

MARIKO B. RYAN

Chapter Eight
Putea Whakairo

PERHAPS NOW WE ARE IN THE PRESENT DAY, AND PERHAPS NOW WE CAN JUMP TO THE INSIGHTS. You are itching. But here I am again coaxing you back to the previous century because while all that kerfuffle was happening in the world of soldiers, scholars, and missionaries, there was a much more intriguing parallel history in motion.

In the 1820s, the missionaries began teaching the natives how to read and write. It was easier to convert them if they could read the scriptures. Many went on to teach their relations, which turned out to be a lucky thing. By the mid-1800s, the sages were becoming increasingly distressed by the impacts of the church on their beliefs—now liberally sprinkled with bits and bobs from the white man's religion. Conversion rates were picking up. The priests began classing certain traditional practices as 'evil' and actively asking people to demonise their own who continued to choose it. It was a downward slide to obliteration. The old knowledge would not survive a sustained onslaught, and the sages wanted to curtail it.

So, they mobilised. They put their newly acquired writing skills to use and began recording traditional knowledge into manuscripts. The books represented a reduction in *tapu*—the powerful ethereal essence of *Atua*, the Great Immortals, deities. A poor substitute for their oral system. Common ink on common paper. It was the white man's mechanism by which any person could record misinformation onto paper without proper moderation or authority. It was permanently fixed. It lacked accountability. Their beloved oral traditions were being transitioned to what they considered to be an inferior communication system. It signalled defeat.

The sages' writings became a countrywide movement that continued for around one hundred years. The manuscripts were called *Putea Whakairo*. Despite their concerns, the manuscripts were imbued with *tapu* to protect them against unauthorised access or desecration—deliberate or otherwise. Now, there would be consequences for any breaches. The manuscripts were well hidden and only passed on to chosen caretakers of subsequent generations for safekeeping—until the 'right person came along'. However, many were afraid to hold them lest they inadvertently break the laws of *tapu*. There were plenty of stories of consequential deaths and ailments to back up their fear. Further, some caretakers were subjected to constant badgering by men desperately wanting the books. No wonder, then, many manuscripts were permanently hidden, buried or burned. The fear and the badgering were too much for many.

The surviving books have become a critical and valuable legacy, but most remained unavailable for too long, and many still are.

This inaccessibility allowed a flood of uncontested academic publications to occupy the shelves. They become the main source of publicly available 'traditional' knowledge. And you know that story already.

Does reinvented and erroneous knowledge matter? Aren't cultures and belief systems riddled with inaccuracies? Should we just call it evolution? Don't all cultures and belief systems change over time? Perhaps the answer lies in the drivers behind the changes. Change instigated by a deliberate colonial strategy of obliteration is not evolution. It is contamination.

MARIKO B. RYAN

Chapter Nine

Complicated Mess

A THORNY PREDICAMENT AWAITED ANYONE WILLING TO SPEND A GOOD PART OF THEIR FUTURE UNTANGLING THIS MESS. No doubt, they would be criticised, chastised, and told they were quite possibly delusional. Cultural elites would peek out from behind clacking laptops and start a pissing contest. Because that's how some of us roll. Conversely, others would say, 'About time', 'You must do this', and 'How can I help?'. Because that's also how some of us roll. Either way, neither of these scenarios should be deterrent or incentive. It is the task that is important, not the reaction that its taskmaster may attract.

By now several years had passed and no-one had emerged as a contender although several had presented themselves in various guises. Some of the wider family and tribe were now asking to understand the knowledge The Old Man had preserved.

I entertained some scenarios. I asked how I might present his work in a way that others could easily benefit. I asked if I had the skills and the tenacity. Did I believe there was enough surviving information and context to retrace and rebuild—to get some value from this legacy? If I sifted through the academic works and their original sources, would I find synergies?

I found the answers to all of these questions in the manuscripts.

So, to the task. I had no plan or process, but looking back, there were four steps. First, I needed to recognise I had a personal interest in the outcome. What I would discover might counter what I'd privately or publicly endorsed, and what I'd been brought up to believe and, in some cases, fear. We cannot work with material we fear. So, I put great effort into putting my beliefs temporarily to the side. Second, when I triangulated information from multiple independent and checked sources, and found the results to be consistent, I got closer to confirming whether the information was authentic. Conversely, when thoroughly and independently examining information that couldn't be triangulated—an anomaly or outlier—then I would not yet consider it credible. Patterns began to appear. Third, if I followed the threads of well-sourced and well-evidenced information, I expected to seamlessly track them to other credible information. A break in those threads occurred if one piece of evidence did not move easily to the next. I began to discover the strong links and the weak. Last, I brought my beliefs back into the centre and reviewed whether I still needed them. I was surprised at how many I could let go, without any sense of pain or loss. Instead, I felt freedom.

The more logical and analytical methods of authenticating knowledge may not appeal to those of you who prefer a solely intuitive or spiritual approach. After all, you will find the insights in this book often encourage it. However, I reminded myself that our old navigators, weavers, astronomers, battle strategists, and agriculturists employed a good measure of analytical, logical, and intellectual know-how alongside the intuitive and spiritual. They perceived no division between them in the way we do today. The mind 'knows', and the heart 'realises'. When both are engaged, stuff happens.

MARIKO B. RYAN

Chapter Ten
Not A Single Tooth

I MIX THE TWO LANGUAGES AS IF I HAVE NO CARE THAT I TOSS SOME OF YOU INTO AN ALTERNATIVE UNIVERSE. Further, *ka huri atu ahau ki te reo rangatira o nga tupuna* without warning. Oh yes. There's going to be a bit of language switching coming up. English and *Te Reo Rangatira*, the Language of Chiefs, will be competing for prime real estate on these pages. Don't worry. I include the meanings either directly before or after the texts, and now and then I do it cryptically, and the explanations may differ a little from the previous ones. I'm not a dictionary, so I indulge in variation to help you understand that a wider contextual playground exists. I hope you will catch the intent and not wish to be spoon-fed.

The verbatim texts in our native language are directly from the manuscripts. The words of The Old Man and his kin transport us to their worlds and times, and so, as we say, they are with us now as we read. Some of the linguistically vigilant amongst you may notice the Maori words are not modernised. You may suggest I have introduced typographic errors, omitted macrons, and used incorrect words. Don't be distracted. I promise, I quadruple-checked every letter, space, and punctuation mark to ensure they were transferred accurately to these pages. The language style is well over one hundred years old and some hundreds more. Some is classical. Some colloquial. Some dialectal. And some, you will not find in any modern 'Maori for Beginners' textbook.

The texts in English are my interpretations. They are based on extensive research and inquiry—including scouring the old unpublished manuscripts in library basements around the country, conversations with several of my elders and others, and of course, The Old Man's manuscripts. Yet, unlocking the meanings was not a straight-forward translating task because worldviews are embedded in the language. It was necessary to delve into the contexts and consciousness of the writers. So, I interpret with a lofty goal in mind—that is, to honour the essence and intent of the original materials and their writers. Those of you who like to thoroughly explore everything will perhaps champion my efforts and sink blissfully into your cushions, book in hand. The rest of you will skate rapidly past my carefully crafted words at blinding speed with nought but a glance.

Despite the language divide between the vowel-laden rhythmic language of the Maori, and the consonant-laden, functional language of the English, I approach the task as poetry, listening as much to the sounds and rhythms of the words as to their meanings. I attempt to echo the style of the storytellers— verbose, raw, symbolic, metaphorical, cryptic, humorous, and hearty. I sometimes mimic the way the orators speak and sometimes how my elders spoke. Thick accents, like earth, streams, sky—the sound of *Aroha*, love unending, unbounded.

Or those of the elders even further back in time, whom my elders loved to impersonate. Drawing their lips as far over their teeth as they could, as if they had not a single tooth left, then speaking with gummy inflection until we were hysterical with laughter. And a few who didn't need to impersonate, back when false teeth were only for rich white folk. It saddens me that many of you will never hear those voices. So instead, I hope you will fall in love with their words purely as a consequence of your imagination.

MARIKO B. RYAN

Chapter Eleven
Nitty-Gritty

THE OLD MAN DID NOT WRITE FOR THE CONVENIENCE OF SCHOLARS THOUGH MANY SWARM ALL OVER THIS KIND OF MATERIAL PERHAPS BELIEVING THEY ARE SOLELY ABLE AND ENTITLED. There were no learners in mind when he considered his future readers. He rarely provided explanations. He was not commissioned or paid to produce the manuscripts. They were for another generation of able sages and descendants, in an unknown future time. He likely assumed future knowledge-keepers would be selected from among the most learned and wise of his descendants, and that their contextual knowledge would be more than sufficient. But colonisation jettisoned contextual knowledge too. Generations came and went. The distances between his assumptions and reality grew wider and wider. Now, even the best of our knowledge leaders critically debate each other's interpretations until there is barely any agreed ground upon which to thrust the stake. Some quietly go about their sage-business. Some claim to have the secrets but won't tell. Some offer their expertise for a hefty price. Some pronounce they are sages searching for devotees. And some offer themselves as husbands.

The manuscripts reveal a universal ideology that is not so easy to interpret without context and a deeper understanding of the language. As the years pass, it becomes progressively more difficult because we lose the direct connections to those who lived during those times, with their context and stories. The generation after mine are too young to have the advantage of direct connections to The Old Man through the tales told by my elders, who were youngsters and teens when he was alive.

I was fortunate to sit with them without expectations or hurry until soon the accumulation of years of dust was brushed off their stories, and countless shining gems were pulled out for me to see. Between my elders and theirs, and all of us, this book captures four or five generations of contexts, explanations, and observations. Sadly, some have now passed on. *Haere ki o tatou tini whanaunga, ka taka i tua o nga puke ra e noho wairua ai. Haere, haere, haere.*

The resulting insights are the nitty-gritty. They peel back the layers of confusion and distractions that pile up when we are inundated with more information than we can process—and when that information lacks wisdom. When we stumble under the weight of too much data and not enough discernment, the insights may lead us out and into a place where clarity and more awareness of our responsibilities and potential seem more accessible. Mostly, they ask us to honour the true nature of our bonds to each other and everything else. To restore our connections. To restore our wisdom.

The insights are the voices of our old people—simultaneously kind, blunt, challenging, indifferent, cheeky, urging.

We don't know from one insight to the next whether to step into an embrace—or flinch! Oh, such is the charm of our old people's voices.

Chapter Twelve
I Write Because

I WRITE BECAUSE THEY WROTE. They wrote because they had something important to say. Certain people came into my life when they needed to and prised opened my eyes.

They taught me that before the answers, there are important questions. That a quiet disposition speaks volumes. That freedom starts inside. Some of them have now gone, and my heart breaks because their loss was a loss to all of us. *Moe mai ra e nga hoa, e nga rangatira.*

I write because we are in a crisis. We are falling, and we need to be caught. There is something we've misplaced. It came out of the mouths of the wisest of my ancestors—and quite possibly yours too. Fortunately, mine left manuscripts behind, knowing that in the throes of colonisation we would one day need to hear their voices. Some of their words are wrenchingly beautiful. Laced with insights. No words wasted.

The insights are seeded by those words. They reveal the best and worst of human nature. I fancy I possess many of the same failings and hypocrisies they reveal, but then the insights give me a chance to restore myself. They ask for empathy, respect, and *Aroha*, love unending, unbounded. Perhaps, none of us truly knows whether we are capable of any of it.

But they help us realise we are equipped with the ability to fill the space between what we know and what we might know—it's a journey we can take together.

My purpose in writing this book is grounded in a simple task. To convey the insights to whoever might feel inspired. It means uncovering some of what was hidden by my people and offering a broader spectrum of knowledge to the world to help inform the choices we make for our descendants.

We do not need hope and faith in some distant being to solve the serious problems we've made and face. We need clarity, conviction, and foresight. And action. We don't need to surrender our personal power to those who do not treasure us. We need to take it back. We don't need to live in a haze of ignorance. We need to shine a light on our greatest questions and find answers. This is not just for my Grandchildren. But for all Grandchildren. I write because we are Kin.

SECTION 1: RITUALS OF ENCOUNTER

Insight 1: Tae-a-tinana. Show Up.

1. Today, you convinced yourself to show up.

2. Willing to be scrutinised. To go down. To get back up.

3. You worry you did not bring your wits, but I see they are about you.

4. You are ready.

5. Should the howling winds of *Tawhirimatea* blow, you will grip with both hands to your centre pole.

6. If, instead, his tropical breezes brush lightly across your skin, you will reach out, gather all you can, and scatter it widely to fill our collective baskets.

7. You promise not to be self-serving, power-mongering or judgemental.

8. After all, you know too well your short-comings and how much further you have to go.

9. Indeed, there were times you were forced to your knees by flawed thinking.

10. Lurching through life.

11. Chastised one minute, uplifted the next.

12. You are giddy.

13. Bear with me.

14. You will know if I am speaking to you directly.

15. You may brace yourself and invite the full force of my words into places inside you that thrive on pain or resistance.

16. Or you will bear witness.

17. I will shower you with love. You will blossom.

18. Then, I will lean in and rattle your foundations with all my might—and promise to catch you should you fall just as others have caught me.

19. We will walk together into my world—my surreal universe—where we will begin the reset.

20. And you will whisper, 'What is this place?'.

Insight 2: Te Waharoa. The Gateway.

21. It begins wherever you are.

22. You linger outside the gateway for the *Karanga*, the Call.

23. You hope, at least, for an affectionate reception—and at most, for revelations of world-changing proportions.

24. You glance nervously at your companions.

25. You have no wish to walk through alone, but you will if you must—for they may not have the courage to

leave the flock, and you are not willing to be mustered towards your future demise.

26. You straighten your skirt, your jacket, your tie, your fringe, your nerves.

27. As if that matters.

28. You shuffle to indicate to those on the other side you are ready—a *nukunuku nekeneke*, a little sideways movement, until you are in full view.

29. Once you pass through, there is no retreat and no return, you will not be able to retrace your steps, nor erase what you have glimpsed.

30. Even so, you do not care to remain in the dysfunction on this side of the gateway.

31. It has come to no good.

32. Wait. Let me place this *Korowai*, this Ornate Woven Feather Cloak, around your shoulders.

33. It will shelter you from the chilly winds of disorder.

34. It is ancient. It is imbued.

35. Every thread in the fabric is stitched with *Aroha*, Authentic Love, and *Whanaungatanga*—Kinship.

36. It holds you. We hold you.

37. Even if the harsh voices of the old people echo.

38. Even as you flinch. Especially as you flinch.

39. Even if your world tumbles.

40. Listen. You discern the *Karanga* now, the distant call to enter.

41. It is on high where ethereal sounds hover above your normal consciousness.

42. You look for the source, but it emerges out of the mists of *Hine-pukohukohu*, the Realm of the Feminine.

43. You query its intent—as it queries yours.

44. Your stomach turns.

45. Despite your uncertainty you step forward.

46. For no less reason than you wish to be dazzled.

Insight 3: Whakatatare. Scrutiny.

47. You have heeded our call to enter.

48. We are not yet privy to each other's intent.

49. But we have readied the fort for a possible onslaught.

50. And the pigs are tied to the stakes ready to feed those with peaceful guise.

51. Apologies to the vegetable-eaters.

52. You cannot say we are not prepared for all possible outcomes.

53. Oh, but sadly we are confined to paper and ink, or bits and bytes.

54. We cannot in reality exchange food—watercress and pork boiled to smithereens.

55. Or send a volley of projectiles your way in our defence.

56. We cannot exchange words nor gestures.

57. Nor can we share the *Ha*, the Pervading Breath.

58. Still, the *Tupuna*, Ancestors, insist it is proper to satisfy the rituals of encounter and perform the sensitive act of determining our mutual good intentions—or not.

Insight 4: Nga Mate. Pouritanga. Death. Grief.

59. You walk forward slowly, for there is much to consider.

60. The *Tupuna*, Ancestors, speak in old words.

61. *Toea mai ra te ata kia mihi atu au he matua ka taka i tua o nga puke ra.*

62. The breaking dawn is a fleeting moment. It is when we acknowledge the Elders who have fallen beyond the shadowy hills to the place we cannot yet reach.

63. In the manner of our old people, we also stand to acknowledge your departed.

64. We honour their presence and recognise those who have fallen and who now accompany you, their Grandchild, on this occasion.

65. We affirm, we are also connected to them, and all of us are part of the everlasting cycle of renewal and replenishment.

66. This is how we come to weep together.

67. The tears fall freely into the morning dew.

68. Because, we have no choice but to wait until we can once again sit at the feet of our Elders—when we too, fall beyond the shadowy hills.

Insight 5: Karakia Tuatahi. First Invocation.

69. Now the first formalities are done, we go to the next.

70. For our people most certainly are the absolute best at drawing out the rituals of encounter.

71. This handshake, quick hello and cheek-pecking procedure will not do—it just will not.

72. How will that lead us to an enhanced appreciation of our *Whanaungatanga*—Kinship?

73. The Old Man provides us with the next formality.

74. Its purpose is to harness the powers of the universe and to set us upon our journey

75. *Na te pukapuka whitu o te Tohunga, wharangi 124. Karakia ite haerenga roa.*

76. From the seventh manuscript of the Sage, page 124. Invocation for the long journey.

77. *Papa te Whatitiri*

78. *Rapa te Uira*

79. *Kapakapatu ana te Rangi e iri iho nei*

80. *Nukuhia a Nuku*

81. *Nukuhia a Rangi*

82. *Kia watea mai a Taihoronukurangi*

83. *Kia tirohia atu te uru o Tangaroa*

84. *E tu mai nei hikihiki Rangi kite tauihu rape nui o Taane*

85. *I tutakina ai te Po uriuri, te Po tangotango, te kapiti rangi*

86. *Ko Tane i wahia mai ai tapuae*

87. Hail, *She* who wields thunderous might

88. Who reverberates midst the lightening barbs

89. The brilliant shafts of the Ancients

90. Yet to expose the prophecy in its fullness

91. Where our foretold path summons

92. The skies, suspended from above

93. Endure the burden of their celestial duty

94. Their divine vaults collide to illuminate the way

95. Extend, Earth Mother! Stand aside, Sky Father!

96. Clear the trail of the One who Connects the Tides and the Skies

97. The horizon ignites, bidding us to seek out the far reaches of the Great Ocean

98. Arise, Sky Father!

99. Arise before the tattooed breech, the sacred Canoe of the Immortals

100. Strike into the intense night, into the palpable night

101. Finally, the skies are one

102. And *Tane* has marked the trail

103. … Fragments of trepidation are cast aside

104. No more are we shore-bound

105. It is time to embark onwards

106. To bind our footprints to distant lands

Insight 6: Kotahi Mano nga Mihi. A Thousand Greetings.

107. I speak a thousand greetings.

To the Great Immortals, to the Eternal Universe, and to the Multitudes

To the Immense Sky and the Glorious Earth

To the Great Weaver of the Sacred Tapestry

To the Thunder and to the Lightning

To the men and women who wore the Cloak of the Sage

To the ancient Knowledge-Keepers

To the Elegant Orators

To the Ancestors and to the Grandchildren

To you whose love has no bounds

To you who seeks the truth

To you who believes and to you who does not

To you who stands to be counted

To you who speaks out

To you who is lost and to you who is found

To you who cannot see and to you who has seen too much

To you who fights for us and to you who fights against

To the enemies and to the allies

To the fallen and to the victorious

To you who occupies the Infinite Genetic Thread

The Sacred Tapestry that connects us all, to us all

The winds blow

They gather

Our intentions are concentrated

And in the manner of our people, I greet you once, twice, and finally thrice.

Insight 7: Mihi. Acknowledgements.

108.   I turn to acknowledgements.

109.   *Te Ira Atua*, the genetic thread of the extended family of the Great Immortals, unfurls.

110.   They are the immense powers of the cosmos, sky, earth, sun, winds, oceans, forests, mountains—deities, gods, whatever you will.

111.   First, to the Parent Immortals, Earth and Sky, who bore the progeny and spawned the founding threads of supernatural beings.

112.   There are many.

113.   Once they have sprung from the topmost threads, the next unfurling occurs.

114.   It is *Te Ira Tangata*, the genetic thread of human beings.

115.   And now, I acknowledge our *Tupuna*, Ancestors, yours and mine.

116.   They marked *Te Ara,* the Trails, and left indelible footprints.

117.   I acknowledge the gifted men and women who conveyed the deep knowledge through millennia.

118.   The *Tohunga*, Sages.

119.   I acknowledge the *Matauranga*, Wisdom, cherished and guarded in the old *Wananga*, Knowledge Sessions.

120.   The elegant compositions spoken by the *Kaikorero*, Orators.

121.   Words of intention, exhilaration, creation, power.

122.   Inhabited by metaphors, imagery, and symbols, so we can step into their worlds and be awed.

123.   A platform from which we, the Grandchildren, may dive deeply.

124.   I acknowledge those who illuminated the way and marked *Te Ara,* the Trails.

125.   I acknowledge the men and women who fulfilled all that needed to be, to bring us to this very day.

126.   And now I have acknowledged those who came before us, I turn to you—*Tena Ko Koe*, Precious One.

127.   I acknowledge your Ancestors, your People, your Place, your Essence.

128.   And our connection—for are we not all Kin?

129.   I see you are weary, as I am, from life's arduous journey.

130.   So, come, let us find our common ground, entwine our intents and share the load.

131.   For there can be no weaving of the Sacred Tapestry without the Infinite Threads upon which we each stand, coming together.

132.   May we seek to serve our purposes under the mantle of *Aroha*, that which encompasses love, empathy, and kinship.

133.   It is with greater honour, I stand with my Ancestors and yours.

134.   May these words serve their noblest desires for all of us.

135.   Welcome to this place.

SECTION 2: CHANGING PERCEPTION

Insight 8: Kaumatua. Elder.

136. You!

137. The Old Man says.

138. His bent forefinger-knuckle is pointing.

139. At me.

140. So all of his fingertips point back at him.

141. The old people say pointing at someone with the pointy ends of fingers is bad form.

142. We are taught not to accuse anyone without also considering our own potential hypocrisy or responsibility.

143. And I am him and he is me. The fingers say so.

144. We come from the same genetic thread.

145. But that fact escapes me.

146. Instead, my fragile ego has me squirming in my inadequacy until I finally realise it is not an accusation, but a dare.

147. He does not blink. His knuckle-pointing does not waver. He waits for my fire.

148. It takes courage and I have not an inch.

149. Then. Pahhh! I faux-lurch and push the sound out. Then laugh.

150. It is the only way to react to a hard-nosed challenge from an old man who has long passed and who has little patience left.

151. He does not comprehend the namby-pamby we like to indulge in these days.

152. He is not of our times.

153. And namby-pamby has no use in an unkind world where people have no love for us, and where we cannot even find love for ourselves.

154. It has no place when there is work to be done.

Insight 9: Taringa Whakarongo. Listening Ears.

155. *Taringa whakarongo!*

156. Listen up, ears!

157. The *Tupuna*, Ancestors, seek not just our ears.

158. They seek all of our senses.

159. Our heart, our consciousness, all of it, all of us.

160. They want us to listen without resistance, defence, competition or interruption.

161. They ask that we quieten the voice that insists we have heard it before, that it is not possible, or that we don't think they have the right to hold us captive in this moment.

162.   They want us to hear the totality before discarding it.

163.   They want only our silence.

164.   No, they are not asking for just our ears, for they alone will not suffice if we mean to reply when a *Tupuna* asks, *I rongo koe ite wairua?*

165.   They ask us to sense with all of our being, the duplicity of our existence, our sensibility and insensibility, our consciousness and consciousness-suppressed, that which touches us and which is touched, that which is summoned when we are born and set adrift when we depart, that which resides in our heart and our mind, that which collects our tears and laughter, that which is instilled, that which is activated, that which sleeps, that which inhabits our dreams and visions, that which shares the ebb and flow of life's breath, the first and the last, and that which binds us to this Infinite Thread.

166.   Now, Breathe.

167.   *Ae, i rongo ahau ite wairua.*

Insight 10: Tai-horo-nuku-rangi. The Expanse. Horizon.

168.   *Tai-horo-nuku-rangi* is the expanse where Sky and Earth meet—the illusion that is the Horizon.

169.   It represents the visual and spiritual line between that which we know, and that which we don't yet know.

170.   The beyond.

171.   We can know *Tai-horo-nuku-rangi* only from where we stand in this exact moment.

172.   Anything else is unknown.

173.   The *Karakia*, Invocation, draws our attention to *Tai-horo-nuku-rangi* to remind us when we take a single step in any direction, the Horizon shifts.

174.   Something once out of view, hidden, will be revealed.

175.   Our perception will be changed.

176.   So, my friend, there is no need to be struck dumb by the unknown.

177.   Just take a step.

Insight 11: Tupari. Precipice.

178.   You stand at the precipice.

179.   One misstep and you think you will plummet into oblivion.

180.   But you hover, waiting for someone to tell you what to do.

181.   You think I will implore you to step back.

182.   You are wrong.

183.   I say it is time to hurl the part of you that is deluded over this cliff.

184.   There is no physical danger, so there is no need to pray for wings.

185.   Pleading is part of your delusion.

186.   In these islands, *Te Rerenga Wairua* is North towards where the sun burns the brightest.

187.   There is a cliff that rises high above.

188.   And below, two great oceans meet.

189.   The ancient roots of gnarly *Pohutukawa* grip steadfastly to the cliff face halfway down, her branches reach out to catch what may fall.

190.   And below her, waves dash against the black rocks.

191.   The *Tupuna*, Ancestors, say the dearly departed soar above us to this place at great speed.

192.   Then, like you, they stand at the precipice.

193.   They glance Southwards to farewell what they leave behind, but they do not linger.

194.   No long goodbyes.

195.   They simply leap.

196.   They catch the swirling wind currents down to the branch of *Pohutukawa*.

197.   Down they go to plunge into the waters of *Hine-Moana*, Keeper of the Ocean.

198.   Moments later, they emerge to check the ocean trail, to confirm the pathway.

199.   Then they dive.

200.   They go to where the dead assemble.

201.   Some call it *Te Po*, The Great Darkness.

202.   It is where their potential can be revisited. A clean slate.

203.   Let us discard ideas about light being good, darkness being bad, heaven and hell, angels and demons, and all of that.

204.   These are adopted from beliefs that belong elsewhere.

205.   The *Tupuna*, Ancients, say there is an emanating light at the outer edges of *Te Po*, the potential of knowing.

206.   It is where *Maramatanga*, Clarity and Illumination, is found.

207.   Some say *Te Po* is a permanent destination for the dead.

208.   However, the pathway is open.

209.   If you have an inclination to visit, then night is best because the darkness frees our senses from our preoccupation with the material world.

210.   Do not be alarmed. I do not suggest a permanent relocation, my friend, just a visit.

211.   The Old Man speaks.

212.   Ko te po nei kia moea iho, e awhi reinga ana taua oho rawa ake nei ki te ao.

213.   This dreamtime is where we awaken.

214.   The limits of our earthly perceptions are set aside.

215.   Here, we may choose to indulge in an embrace with our departed loved one, or we may choose a substantial awakening of consciousness.

216.   If only we would leap.

Insight 12: Nekehia te Pumahara. Shift Perception.

217.   The ancient *Karakia*, Invocation, is an expectation we will shift our perception from our daily material world to another.

218.   Yet, we would rather hold to what is familiar, safe, and stable.

219.   The sky is above, the ground below, and all is tickety-boo in our world.

220.   We might shift our perspective if forced to by some shock or calamity.

221.   The *Karakia* first requires us to let go.

222.   Second, to summon the Great Immortal Grandmothers on high.

223.   *Te Whatitiri*, Thunder, resounds and *Te Uira*, Lightning, seeks out.

224.   Third, to gaze outwards to *Tai-horo-nuku-rangi*, where *Nuku*, Earth, and *Rangi*, Sky, are clear, and the far reaches of *Tangaroa*, The Great Ocean, are laid out to the horizon.

225.   Fourth, to mark the trail.

226.   The world will be transformed.

227.   Oh, but we did not activate nor witness it.

228.   We were rummaging down at the shoreline, stooping to select pretty shells, chase crabs, and scrunch our toes into the shifting sand.

229.   We only saw the lapping waves and heard the squawks of seagulls.

230.   The *Karakia*, all of the old people's efforts, all of this writing, all of it is perhaps wasted upon one who is not receptive to shifting their perspective after all.

SECTION 3: SOURCE OF KNOWLEDGE

Insight 13: Matauranga. All Knowledge.

231.   The old people ask us to consider this.

232.   All knowledge exists.

233.   What we seek is already knowable.

234.   We do not own it. We do not create it. We cannot contain it.

235.   But we can capture it.

236.   We are merely a conduit by which it arrives, so unless we unblock the entrance, it will not come.

237.   That's fine. Not everybody wants it.

238.   But the *Tohunga*, Sage, welcomes it.

239.   What is within, is without.

240.   You will read the insights about the universe, and discover what happens out there, happens inside us too.

241.   It is all one.

242.   And the *Tohunga* knows this.

243.   In a state of *Te Kore*, The Great Nothingness, there is an infinite emptiness where *knowing* is anticipated.

244.   In a state of *Te Po*, The Unfathomable Darkness, *knowing* is conceived and takes form.

245. In a state of *Te Ao Marama*, The Bright Light of Comprehension, *knowing* appears in fullness.

246. In one moment the *Tohunga*, her eyes closed in contemplation, may sense nothing.

247. In the next, a small feather may drift silently by.

248. The *Tohunga* will suddenly raise her hand and pluck it from the air.

249. *Kapo-wairua.*

250. Eyes still closed.

Insight 14: Te Puna-ite-Ao-Marama. Wellspring of Enlightenment.

251. A story was recorded in the manuscripts by the *Tohunga*, Sage, at the old *Wananga*, Knowledge Sessions.

252. It is the epic tale of the Great Navigator, *Kupe*.

253. Some seventy years before this account, a young *Kupe* left his Pacific island, *Hawaiki-Rangi*.

254. He was in somewhat of a flurry and keen to move things along at speed.

255. There had been a scurrilous incident involving a tryst with his lover *Kura-maro-tini*, her husband *Hoturapa*—and a failed murder.

256.   However intriguing that may sound, we cannot linger there because there is an even greater story to be told than that of an improper romance and ill intent towards a third party.

257.   So we shall hurry along with *Kupe* to tell the story quickly lest he be captured before he has had the chance to leave the shore.

258.   *Kupe* procured his beloved ocean-going *Matawhaorua*, a large double-hulled ocean-going vessel, for his getaway.

259.   He crewed the vessel with his lover, *Kura-maro-tini*, and the strongest of his relations, convincing them to start a new life in the mystical land beyond the horizon.

260.   He used the most powerful *Karakia*, Invocations, he knew to harness the powers of the Great Immortals to help him escape this predicament.

261.   He marked *Te Ara*, the trail across *Te Moana-nui-a-Kiwa*, the Great Ocean of Kiwa, the Pacific Ocean.

262.   *Kupe* and his people set out never to return.

263.   Many days later, they reached *Te-Ika-a-Maui*, the North Island of Aotearoa.

264.   They came ashore in the *Hokianga*—a harbour with a perilous bar, flanked by gigantic sand dunes reflecting the sun's rays back up to the Southern sky.

265.   His people settled, produced offspring, and flourished.

266.   Many decades later, *Kupe* became nostalgic for home.

267.   He yearned to return to *Hawaiki-Rangi* to live his final days.

268.   However, his people did not want him to abandon them.

269.   To prove he was still committed to his people in *Aotearoa*, he promised to leave his son *Tuputupu-whenua*.

270.   However, the boy did not want to stay. He insisted he leave with his father. He would not be moved.

271.   *Kupe* had no choice but to enforce the matter.

272.   In the morning, he enticed *Tuputupu-whenua* to the famous Spring, *Te Puna-ite-Ao-Marama*, the Wellspring of the World of Enlightenment.

273.   It flows out from the edge of the dunes on the northern side of the harbour.

274.   Here in the manuscripts, the *Tohunga* chooses not to write the exact process of what happened next.

275. That knowledge, he insists is *Tapu*, under the influence of the Great Immortals, and is not for common people. So he summarises.

276. After feigning a farewell to his son, *Kupe* promptly recited a strong *Karakia*, Invocation.

277. He drank three times from the Spring and farewelled it too.

278. He said.

279. *Hei konei ra, e Te Puna-ite-Ao-Marama.*

280. *Ka hoki anganui ake nei tenei, e kore ano e hoki anga nui mai.*

281. This is a departure. There will be no coming back.

282. Then he abruptly cast his son *Tuputupu-whenua* into the Spring where he was transformed into a *Taniwha*, a Supernatural Guardian.

283. Some say the Spring is the source of all Enlightenment.

284. Some say the story is a fable.

285. Some say it is just a place where *Kupe* happened to see the water-like reflection of sunlight on golden sand.

286. All I say is the home people continue to protect *Te Puna-ite-Ao-Marama* to this day.

287. And *Tuputupu-whenua* still holds vigil.

288.   It is rare to take visitors there for fear of desecration.

289.   The shifting sands change the landscape constantly.

290.   The Spring hides in plain view amongst others that gush out from the inner crevices below the dunes.

291.   You will not find it.

Insight 15: Whakatuturu. Whakarite. Triangulate.

292.   He aha te mea tika?

293.   We are gullible.

294.   We scour the news and disinformation designed to feed our fears, our excitement for conspiracies, our desire for drama.

295.   We are sucked in by clever liars who are intent on furthering their aspirations for power and control.

296.   The truth has become so elusive we either believe nothing or everything, and trust is out the window.

297.   We share our discoveries widely—our friends need to know! The world needs to know!

298.   We become entrenched, protecting our reputations even when evidence to the contrary begins to emerge.

299.   Even when our friends gently tell us we have been tricked.

300.   The heels are most surely digging in, and we will not be moved.

301.   The instigators are amused because we are so easily duped. It is child's play.

302.   Let us tease this out, so we can find some clarity.

303.   This is not a modern-day phenomenon. It has been going on forever.

304.   When told to believe something, we must surely check before adopting it as our truth.

305.   Triangulate. Corroborate. Dig deeper.

306.   It's where sleuthing and common sense come together.

307.   If we cannot convince our sceptical selves, our objective selves, or our detached selves, then perhaps we have elevated our desire to confirm some existing belief we like to hold on to.

308.   Perhaps we want to appease someone whose approval is important to us.

309. Perhaps one truth will undo a mistruth, and another, and we cannot take the slow motion destruction of our worldview.

310. The old people show us that knowledge and wisdom are constants.

311. It should be easy to confirm how one piece of information is connected to another.

312. No missing pieces. Not square peg, round holes.

313. All fitting together neatly to show us the entirety.

Insight 16: Ehara ite Matauranga Tawhito. Knowledge is not Ancient.

314. Here we are!

315. Born of cascading generations of shrinking nobility.

316. Reduced to thin receptacles by the systematic suppression of ancient knowledge in favour of modern-day frippery.

317. We possess all the knowledge of a hee-hawing ass.

318. Maybe less. I disrespect the ass.

319. There is much more information in our heads than our *Tupuna*, Ancestors, ever had.

320.   Yet, we somehow know we are a duller version of them.

321.   We crave authentic, substantial knowledge to supersede the garbage we are fed.

322.   But who will supply it now the *Tohunga Tuturu*, True Sages, have expired?

323.   We call upon the modern self-proclaimed *Tohunga* with their modern-day communication devices, social media accounts, and smooth marketing.

324.   Some believe their delusions—their guruhood.

325.   Others are walking wounded, feeling competent through life experience to help their embattled comrades, while refusing help for themselves.

326.   Some are just smooth operators.

327.   Gurus in every city in every country. Guru tourism. It's a thing.

328.   Foreigners and white folk flock to their handsome brown exoticness and slow, steady gaze.

329.   Filling their pockets with money and accolades.

330.   Looking for enlightenment. For release. The search is real.

331.   The exhilaration is real too—in the moment—but does it not dwindle in the subsequent weeks?

332. Really, what do any of us know about True Sages?

333. If the old people were here, they would simply ask whether the gurus can replicate the powers and *Mana* of the old Sages.

334. Can they command the celestial Grandmothers to wield thunderous might and reverberate amidst the lightning barbs?

335. Can they command the Oceans to rise up and carry a sacred vessel safely to new lands in just a tenth of the time normally taken?

336. Can they transform themselves and others into Creatures to guard lairs or scuttle along skirting boards?

337. Let us simplify this.

338. Let us take control of our knowledge.

339. Understand we cannot have all of our questions indulged.

340. This is not a how-to guide.

341. I don't want your dependency.

342. I do want your courage and commitment.

343. Wait. I admit I have told you a lie.

344. Ancient knowledge is not ancient.

345. It is now. It is retrievable. And we can put it to good use.

346.   It is released by plunging the *Toki*, Adze, into the fabric of our (un)reality.

347.   What rushes through the rupture may be an abundance of brilliant insights for the sincere learner, or an outpouring of nonsensical fantasies for the self-absorbed and superstitious.

348.   So, let us not go like fools.

349.   Katahi nei te poro heahea ko koe!

350.   The *Tohunga* says, *Na te waewae i kimi*, the seeking feet.

351.   The diligent seeker will find it.

352.   And does not trot in like a blundering ass!

Insight 17: Hinengaro. Mind.

353.   We are sure deep knowledge is located somewhere.

354.   If only it would reveal itself.

355.   We stare at the night sky. Ask *Rehua* for his ancient knowledge, but we blink and miss the shooting star.

356.   We climb the mountain. Ask *Tawhiri-matea* for his ancient knowledge, but he just ruffles our hair.

357.   We kneel by the rock. Ask *Kohatu* for her ancient knowledge, but suspect she is not listening, for she makes no gesture at all.

358.   We walk the forest. Ask *Tane-mahuta* for his ancient knowledge, but only hear the rustling leaves.

359.   We conclude this deeper knowledge hides.

360.   But, hiding is not the same as being lost.

361.   One is proactive in its concealment.

362.   The other waits to be found.

363.   We are looking in the wrong places.

364.   Instead, look where lost things wait.

365.   In places we've been missing, avoiding, ignoring.

366.   Move whatever is in the way—including our scepticism.

367.   Deeper knowledge drifts in and alights. There.

368.   It is *Hine-ngaro*, *Hine,* the Feminine, *Ngaro,* undetected, unnoticed, unseen—the Unseen Mind. Our reflections. Our contemplations. Our intuitions. Our meditations.

Insight 18: Tirohia-a-Wairua. Consciousness Reality.

369. Long ago, the Great Navigator *Kupe* and his ocean-going double-hulled canoe *Matawhaorua* made the return voyage from *Aotearoa*, across the Great Ocean of *Kiwa*, *Te-Moana-Nui-A-Kiwa*, the Pacific Ocean.

370. *Kupe* desired to live his remaining days in his cherished homeland, *Hawaiki-Rangi*.

371. Following an unfortunate series of local conflicts, his grandson *Nukutawhiti* asked *Kupe* if he and his crew could follow the trail he had marked out. To *Aotearoa*. To start anew. Very soon.

372. Yes, we've been here before.

373. The old man agreed and gifted the younger man his beloved *Waka*, Vessel, named *Matawhaorua*.

374. It was re-adzed to lighten it and increase its holding capacity.

375. Then renamed *Ngatoki-matawhaorua*, re-adzed *Matawhaorua*.

376. Even with the rework, the old *Waka* had already done its share of oceanic journeys.

377. It needed all the powers available to ensure success.

378. Naturally, *Nukutawhiti* and his crew were precious to *Kupe*.

379. So he made the vessel *Tapu* to draw upon the influence of not one or two, but several *Atua*, the Great Immortals.

380. The human crew comprised those particular *Tohunga* who would administer the otherworldly essentials for a safe voyage.

381. Also, the strongest and ablest men and women who would easily endure the voyage.

382. Oh, some of you spotted a possible error.

383. Have we not been told many times in recent years there were no women onboard *Ngatoki-matawhaorua* because of a woman's (so-called negative) power to render the *Tapu* ineffectual?

384. Allow me to lay down another proposition.

385. The manuscripts insist *Kupe* only had one stipulation to protect the *Tapu,* as we shall note shortly.

386. It was not to ensure the absence of women.

387. In certain states and conditions women, as with men, carry the *Tapu*.

388. Colonisation, convenience, and indoctrination have erased them from the accounts.

389.   I'm putting them back in the *Waka*.

390.   How else will the progeny be produced?

391.   And where should we put she who occupies the heart of *Nukutawhiti*, that is his love *Kahu-ote-Rangi*. Strapped to a raft at the back?

392.   In making the *Waka* so *Tapu*, *Kupe* needed to impose some extraordinary conditions and restrictions lest it be diminished.

393.   The vessel would not carry food as it was considered mundane and would potentially negate any supernatural powers—if so, said *Kupe*, the *Waka* would be destroyed.

394.   However, the crew would not survive weeks of oceanic travel without food, so the journey needed to be shortened to just a few days.

395.   Unlike *Karakia*, Invocations normally recited to ensure fair seas, this *Karakia* was to bring about rough seas.

396.   *Kupe* summoned a swell that would advance across the ocean at great speed.

397.   It was called *Ngaru-nui*, the Great Wave.

398. *Tirohia-A-Wairua* is when we dream or perceive another consciousness and our realities become fused and indistinguishable.

399. *Tirohia-A-Wairua* allows us to observe the extraordinary and ordinary at the same time.

400. Anything is possible.

401. Eventually, when forced to re-enter the material world, we feel we are losing our freedom.

402. We are.

403. Sadly, the thin veil between is inevitably snatched away because we must return to our day-to-day lives.

404. Even though they confine us to the time and space of our narrow perceptions.

405. The *Tohunga*, Sage, speaks.

406. *Te ahua nei kite tirohia-a-wairuatia atu te haere mai a taua waka i penei inga ika paapahu e auheke mai nei i roto ite ngaru.*

407. In this state of consciousness, the manner of the journey is likened to a dolphin surfing the wave.

408. The magnificent vessel *Ngatoki-matawhaorua* 'is' the dolphin.

409. The intention of the *Karakia* is not from some place out there to be tapped by some kind of external magic.

410. The intention of the *Karakia* is from within us. We create.

411. *Tirohia-a-wairua.*

412. *Ngaru-nui* reached its destination after just three days and three nights.

413. It released *Ngatoki-matawhaorua* and its crew safely into the watery embrace of the *Hokianga* harbour.

414. *Aotearoa.*

Insight 19: Purakau Whanui. Ancient Stories in Full.

415. The *Purakau*, Ancient Stories, reveal the philosophies and worldviews.

416. The elaborate accounts forge pathways through the labyrinths of our diverse realities.

417. They draw in the curious and challenge the intellect.

418. They fortify, confront or alter something within.

419. Oh, some say they meander, go off topic, circle back, or not, and please, please just get to the point.

420.   We are in a hurry and want the key messages dropped at our feet.

421.   So, we reduce stories to soundbites, with one-dimensional characters and standard plot structures by which chapters are swiftly written and sold.

422.   As if we have limited capacity to comprehend any more than simplistic ideas.

423.   They leave us, the listeners, unsatisfied.

424.   Every detail omitted shrinks the profoundness of the culture and philosophy from which the story was originally sourced.

425.   Thin and empty tales create thin and empty people.

426.   Do we not cherish our capacity for intellectual and philosophical endeavour?

427.   Do we not wish to be enticed into the depths and breadths of our imaginations?

428.   Do we not want all of the twists and turns?

429.   When we pause to digest the seemingly unfathomable, will we not feel invigorated and grateful for the time spent?

430.   *Te kupu i whakaheia ki runga o Maramarama-ite-rangi.*

431.   Let the stories be well lit in the broad daylight.

SECTION 4: PROTECTING KNOWLEDGE

Insight 20: Whakahaumaru e Toru. Three Layers of Protection.

432.   Those who attended *Wananga*, the old Knowledge Sessions, pledged secrecy.

433.   The *Tohunga*, Sage, shrank from any ideas of disclosure to the uninitiated.

434.   This was the first stronghold of protection to curb misuse or contamination of the knowledge.

435.   It would ensure *Tangata Kuware*, Incompetents, would not pollute it with inaccuracies and half-truths.

436.   That *Tangata Matapiko*, Scoundrels, would not use it for selfish or malevolent intents.

437.   And even if revealed, too many would not know the proper use of it. Its true power.

438.   So, only the chosen *Tauira*, the Meticulous Ones, would be trained to hold it.

439.   The second protection was afforded by the *Tapu*.

440.   This enigmatic essence was sourced from *Atua*, the Great Immortals.

441.   *Tapu* was imbued into the words.

442.   It regulated unauthorised access.

443.   None would cross it.

444.   In its harshest form, breaching *Tapu* would be punishable by death, and misfortune could be visited upon the offender's descendants.

445.   There was a third protection.

446.   It was the obscure language between *Atua*, Deities, and the true *Tohunga,* of which he or she had perfect knowledge.

447.   And of which common people, colonials, scholars, and eavesdroppers had none.

448.   It enabled the *Tohunga* to communicate esoteric concepts in private.

449.   We may ask, why so well guarded with these three layers of protection?

450.   Of what use is knowledge if only held by so few?

451.   With the knowledge safeguarded, a strict selection of trusted experts could apply it in the way it was meant.

452.   The Healers cured sick people, the Navigators marked the trails, the Agriculturalists scheduled cultivation cycles, the Genealogists safeguarded the genetic lines, and the Seers ensured people were well prepared for future events.

453.   And that, *e hoa ma*, my friends, is just the start.

Insight 21: Reiuru, Rauriki. Secret Ritualistic Language of Tohunga.

454.   The *Tohunga*, Sage, writes about awakening *Kahukura*—the Collective of *Atua*, the Great Immortals.

455.   It is from them all *Tapu* is sourced.

456.   The Sage writes.

457.   *Ka whakaoho te Tohunga ia Kahukura.*

458.   *He mea whakaoho kite reo Reiuru kite reo Rauriki.*

459.   *Ko tenei reo kote reo Reiuru ko tona korero kote reo tino tapu o Papatuanuku.*

460.   *Kote reo Rauriki tona korero kote reo tino tapu o Ranginui.*

461.   The Sage uses *Tapu* language, that is, the secret ritualistic language of the Great Immortals.

462.   *Ko te Reo Reiuru* is the matriarchal language of *Papa-tua-nuku*, Earth Mother and her Immortal Female Offspring.

463.   *Ko te Reo Rauriki* is the patriarchal language of *Rangi-nui*, Sky Father and his Immortal Male Offspring.

464.   The words of *Reiuru* and *Rauriki* are infused with a celestial essence, and so when spoken, the connection with the Great Immortals is established.

Insight 22: Te Reo Inamata. The Ancient Formal Language.

465.   The *Tohunga*, Sage, explains.

466.   His writings cannot be understood by just anyone.

467.   *Ka hohonu tenei ona korero, me tona reo tapu.*

468.   *Maku ano e tohutohu te tikanga o tenei kupu, o tenei kupu.*

469.   He says the complex meanings and traditions of Every Single Word must be explained.

470.   It is the language of those old *Tohunga* who are no longer with us.

471.   It spans back four thousand years, and the language is cryptic.

472.   It conceals much.

473.   It is deeply *Tapu*.

474.   But before he passed, he found no-one suitable to teach because those old days were gone.

475.   Grief.

476.   *Aku kiri kanohi he hanga ki a mapuna te roimata i aku kamo.*

477.   Upon my eyelashes, bubbling forth like water from a spring, are tears from my eyes.

Insight 23: Matauranga Huna. Tangata Rupahu. Untold Knowledge. Imposters.

478.   The latter years, before the last of the old *Tohunga*, Sages, passed, were stained by significant historical events—mementoes from the Colonisers.

479.   The colonial land wars, influenza epidemic, two world wars, religious conversion, urbanisation, bureaucratic apparatuses.

480.   All contributed to the decimation of the *Tohunga* and the alienation of the old knowledge.

481.   So the *Tohunga* relaxed the *Wananga*, Knowledge Sessions, to include more participants—those who would not have been selected in normal circumstances—in the hope that if there were more of them, the chances of the knowledge being held in perpetuity might be raised.

482.   It was a flawed plan, but desperation called.

483.   The *Tohunga* shared basic accounts but considered some knowledge too *Tapu* for this group.

484.   He would not give it to those unable or unwilling to uphold its integrity.

485.   So he left parts untold. Protected.

486.   He said there was no Sage left who could perform the rituals necessary to save him from the penalty of telling secrets to those who were unfit.

487.   Even so, too many men from those sessions began claiming they were fully trained *Tohunga*. Oh yes! Sages everywhere!

488.   They craved an audience. They craved *Mana*, power, potency, prestige.

489.   They had much to say when in gullible company. Mouthpieces of the gods!

490.   But would say little in well-versed company lest the more discerning get a peep at the ass's ear under the Sage's hood.

491.   The old *Tohunga* not wanting to feed these *Tangata Rupahu*, Imposters, anymore, closed the Knowledge Sessions for good.

492.   But they needed only hold steady until they could permanently secure their status—an easy waiting game made possible by the impending departure of the last of the elderly Sages.

493.   When the Imposters would be unleashed.

494.   The Old Man was too old. He was done. He had to let go.

495.   But he was not finished.

496.   It was his last move before the Shadowy Hills called.

497.   His hidden books would remain protected from the Imposters by the *Moko-Kakariki*, the Shapeshifter, the Emerald Green Gecko, and by fear, the *Tapu*.

498.   Protected for a very long time.

499.   Until one day the protection would be lifted.

Insight 24: Hunga Awangawanga. Those Who Doubt.

500.   I do not strive to trample any knowledge held by any Elders—yours or mine.

501.   Their information may be at odds, but I know all too well that it is better to nod and accept our differences than tussle with each other, hoping to win an unwinnable argument.

502.   Hugs not Hurt.

503.   We have been taught to respect our Elders, but we worry.

504.   They have told us things, always with *Aroha*, with a deep devotion, but they sometimes disagree amongst themselves about who holds the truth.

505.   A long time ago, knowledge was held by those far more learned than today's Elders. Their Ancestors.

506.   Most of the Elders from recent generations have not benefited from the continuous, strict succession of knowledge.

507.   Theirs was interrupted by colonisation, disease, war, religion, busy lives, the loosening of the truth from its roots.

508.   Some of them are well read and can impart the knowledge from academic books.

509.   No wonder you hear inconsistencies.

510.   We may secretly doubt those whom we should respect unconditionally.

511.   The idea that Elders must never be questioned is a remnant of a time when the ancient *Tohunga,* Sages, were the chosen and mandated Knowledge-Keepers.

512.   They developed rigorous systems to ensure knowledge survived intact for untold generations.

513.   It was a critical system of a highly-developed oral culture.

514.   But by the 1800s, they began adopting the Coloniser's written word as the vehicle for truth. A compromise. My compromise too.

515.   Some wrote for the Coloniser scholars—with creative modifications.

516.   Some wrote unsolicited manuscripts for their descendants.

517.   These *Tohunga* spoke while the *Kaituhi*, Scribe, wrote.

518.   Then the *Kaiwhakarongo*, Witnesses, scratched their signatures to confirm the written records were accurate.

519.   Now they could be passed to future generations with confidence.

520.   Falsifying information was not a consideration in these Sessions.

521.   Once witnessed, authenticated, and confirmed, the spoken words were fixed.

522.   Even though the paper separated the knowledge from *Te Ha,* the Pervading Breath, they were, and still are, considered to be *Tapu* words.

523.   That is, influenced by and sourced from *Atua*, the Great Immortals.

524.   To challenge them was an insult to the Sage and those who witnessed the records many generations prior.

525.   But by the mid-1900s, the influence of the Colonisers' values was endemic.

526.   The Knowledge Sessions continued, but now, some were modifying the knowledge for personal, political or religious purposes.

527.   Others, whose learning had been interrupted, were sharing incomplete knowledge without an understanding of its proper application.

528.   Others abandoned rigour in favour of a lax and lazy approach.

529.   And others sanitised the accounts to appease the sensitivities of their Colonial friends—censoring the raw stories that might otherwise further reduce the Colonial opinion of our people.

530.   The old Sages felt immeasurable sadness.

531.   They would baulk at what was later claimed to be authentic.

532.   Later, there were those who received knowledge in good faith. Our Elders.

533.   To challenge information is still considered to be an affront to the Elder providing it, and by association, his or her Elders—even when its accuracy may have been compromised.

534.   Even so, it does us no favours to accept something as fact without proper scrutiny.

535.   Broken threads everywhere.

536.   It weakens our intellectual and spiritual foundation.

537.   It results in the loss of authentic accounts, devalues the knowledge and reduces the benefit from knowing it.

538.   It is a fight to have authentic knowledge heard amongst the din.

539.   And the teller of a tale may never accept theirs may be wrong. Oh no. It came directly from their Elder.

540.   Or better, they read it in a book written by a Coloniser scholar, who gleaned it from a friendly native, who told it to them in strict confidence. No less.

541.   This is all a part of our historical reality. It is for us to navigate.

542.   Our doubts can be a quiet reflection and a steadfast determination to seek what is meaningful to us.

543.   What we pass on to others is a choice.

544.   The deepest of all knowledge is universal, and we can find our way back to it.

545.   In the words of The Old Man.

546.	*E noho nei whakamau kau atu ai tana manawa katoa ki nga tupuna.*

547.	*Aroha mau tonu e kore nei e nukuhia, e kore e nekehia.*

548.	Yes, we can still have unwavering love for our Elders—even when we don't believe their words.

Insight 25: Takahia Matauranga. Undermining Knowledge.

549.	In rare accounts, the *Tupuna*, Ancestors, tell of their sorrow.

550.	It took just a few decades for the knowledge to be toppled under the punitive conditions of colonisation.

551.	The *Tohunga*, Sages, were disarmed.

552.	Outsiders were meddling.

553.	They were compelled because of historical circumstances to write their knowledge into manuscripts.

554.	So, the *Tohunga* and *Kaituhi*, Scribes, coordinated to carefully preserve the secrets in writing.

555.	If they could have continued to orally pass it to their successors, in the way of the old people, they would certainly have done so.

556. Those who wrote neither for money nor to appease academic institutions, churches or politicians had a single focus.

557. That is, to ensure the authentic knowledge would be safeguarded for their descendants who, they expected, would one day benefit from the legacy.

558. Anguish grips tightly to their words.

559. It is like defeat. Sorrow.

560. Yet, it must now dissipate because we, the naïve *Mokopuna*, Grandchildren, for whom they prepared, have finally arrived.

561. It is time, and we have much to do.

562. We wonder how to unlock and honour this knowledge.

563. I tell you, it is not by *Takahia*, trampling over the Sages' work by tainting it with outsider beliefs or agendas or guesswork or whatever-you-fancy.

564. It is not by treating it like faery tales or sorcery.

565. And it is not by burying it with the dead out of misplaced fear.

Insight 26: Hokinga Mai o nga Mokopuna. Return of the Grandchildren.

566.   It is over two hundred years since the beginning-of-the-end of our ancient followings.

567.   The old *Tohunga*, Sages, wrote for the continuation of knowledge so you, their *Mokopuna*, their Progeny, could stay properly embedded in *Te Ira Atua* and *Te Ira Tangata*, the Infinite Threads that connect us.

568.   Those old *Tohunga* did not know so many of their precious *Mokopuna* would eventually adopt others' beliefs as a crutch for their spiritual malnourishment.

569.   If they had, they would no doubt ask us to call our people back home.

570.   The essence of ancient knowledge can still be found, even in the dwindling light, but it won't shine in its full splendour until the *Mokopuna* return.

Insight 27: Te Wa Whakapuaki. Time to Reveal.

571.   It is said the knowledge of the *Tohunga*, Sage, must be held in absolute secrecy, for enemies lurk in shadows and we, *Tangata Hangenge*, the Feeble Ones, must not know it.

572.   There are secrets for the benefit of all, and there are those that are mischief for Mischief-Makers.

573.   But now, we have arrived at the rotten edge of our existence where our choices have been so destructive, for so long, we have finally exposed the edge of the abyss.

574.   Be assured, the Mischief-Makers are already armed.

575.   So.

576.   Is it time to reveal the Sage's secrets?

577.   If not now.

578.   Then when?

MARIKO B. RYAN

SECTION 5: BEYOND THE MATERIAL WORLD

Insight 28: Nga Mea Whakatangitangi. Sound.

579. It is in *Te Po*, the Unfathomable Darkness, that sound first manifests.

580. Sound occurs even before the emergence of *Te Ao Marama*, The Emerging Light.

581. What is without, is within.

582. The genealogy of sound begins with *Te Kune*, the Swelling, and *Te Tupu*, the Growth.

583. It is pushed into the world with *Te Hotupuu*, the Gasping, *Te Kareraa*, the Calling Out, and *Te Tioro*, the Anguish.

584. Then comes *Te Mita*, The Pulse of everything.

585. *Nga Ao*, the worlds, the universes, the realms, the dimensions, us.

586. We know these sounds, do we not?

587. What is without, is within.

Insight 29: Te Mita. The Pulse.

588. Sound, a means by which the *Tohunga*, Sage, gains admission to the realm of *Atua*, the Great Immortals.

589.   When the *Tohunga* desires to transform the mundane into the extraordinary by harnessing the collective powers of the Great Immortals, he or she recites the *Karakia*, Invocation, out loud.

590.   It is a long, rapid monotone.

591.   It is vibration. It is *Mita*. It is Pulse.

592.   The recital is designed to synchronise with the *Mita* of the Great Immortals.

593.   At first they may be mismatched, but soon they come together.

594.   Now the two are indiscernible.

595.   The *Mita* is everywhere.

596.   You may only hear the drone of a monotonous voice, but I hear the thrum of an incredible multi-layered soundscape.

Insight 30: Te Kore. The Nothingness.

597.   Our people say *Te Kore* is Nothingness.

598.   It is before anything and everything; definitely before the darkness of *Te Po*, the Potential, and certainly before *Te Ao Marama*, the Enlightenment.

599.   Even knowledge does not penetrate the great emptiness of *Te Kore*.

600. It is nothing.

601. Nothing is possessed, nothing is felt, nothing cannot be measured or weighed.

602. There is a perception of silence, but even that does not exist.

603. Only one thing has a presence.

604. The *Wairua*, Spiritual Essence, drifts in the great emptiness.

605. The *Tohunga*, Sage, sends forth his intent through *Karakia*, the Invocation, to where the *Wairua* is, so it can be conceived from within *Te Kore*.

606. Out here, we say we can hear his voice reciting.

607. This, we are sure, is not silence. It is not Nothing.

608. It is something.

609. It cannot be *Te Kore* if it is something.

610. Then again, we did not follow his voice to the formless edge of *Te Kore*.

611. If we had, we would have most certainly heard nothing—not even the drifting *Wairua*.

Insight 31: Te Po. The Darkness.

612.   The *Tohunga*, Sages, describe the evolving Universe and the encounter with *Te Po*, the Darkness, in great detail.

613.   *I tutakina te Po-nui*, the Great Night, *Te Po-roa*, the Long Night, *Te Po-uriuri*, the Deep Night, *Te Po-kerekere*, the Intense Night, *Te Po-tiwhatiwha*, the Gloomy Night, *Te Po-tangotango*, the Intense Night, and countless more.

614.   As it is in the universe, so too is it within us.

615.   It is the many nights.

616.   It has feeling, it has seeking, it has restlessness.

617.   When the Darkness is not bound by the limitations of our senses, it will be diffused and potential activated.

618.   Likewise, when the internal essence of *You* is not bound by your senses, your Darkness will be diffused and your potential activated.

Insight 32: Te Ao Marama. The Light, Enlightenment.

619.   We move through three phases. The first two, *Te Kore*, the Great Nothingness, the infinite emptiness

where *knowing* is conceived; to *Te Po*, the Unfathomable Darkness, where *knowing* emerges.

620.   Then on to the last phase *Te Whai-Ao,* the glimmer of dawn, and *Te Ao Marama*, the Light, that is, Enlightenment where *knowing* manifests.

621.   Oh, it is far too ethereal for us!

622.   We claim the width and breadth of the universe is evidentially perceived by our limited senses and experience—smell, sight, touch, and the rest.

623.   If it is claimed that our senses are inadequate, we cry, *Show me the evidence!*

624.   Tell me, which of our limited senses should we engage to best perceive this evidence?

625.   What senses should we call upon so *Te Ao Marama*, the Light of Clarity, may penetrate the iron doors of our closed minds?

Insight 33: Atua Wahine. Female Deities.

626.   I'll keep it short or I'll be here all day.

627.   Recently, at the highest of highest levels, a male deity was installed above the male immortal deities, who were installed above the female deities.

628.   He occupies the topmost heaven, the throne room, the penthouse.

629.   The female deities are relegated to the basement, the lower levels of the deity heavens where daintiness, subservience, victimhood, poor intellect, and evil wallow.

630.   Even *Papa-tua-nuku*, Earth Mother, has not escaped. Platitudes are worthless when so much destruction upon her body is tolerated.

631.   Yet, this hierarchy did not exist in the early unsolicited manuscripts of *Tohunga*, the Sages.

632.   Nor was it embedded in the ancient *Karakia,* Invocations.

633.   Put another way, only the manuscripts that were solicited and/or paid for by Colonial scholars supported it—and their credibility, ahem, has been thoroughly cooked.

634.   Still, some thought it a good idea to perpetuate this hierarchy and created a pretty comprehensive backstory to support it.

635.   But threads should always lead to more threads, and if they don't, if they are broken or waving in the breeze, then the Sacred Tapestry will be full of holes.

636.   The result of this positioning for the female deities—and their human counterparts—is invisibility or ill treatment.

637.   So, the more articulate womenfolk asserted they were not being well represented.

638.   They could not see why they should accept yet another all-superior male god into the mix.

639.   To appease them, the uppermost male deity was reframed as gender-neutral—but still somehow clasped to his male attributes, and was still commonly referred to as 'he'.

640.   Nevertheless, the gender-neutral aspect pleased some, and so they ran with it.

641.   Others stood to the side, rolling their eyes.

642.   In another recent version, some kind of female token-like deity has been inserted alongside this superior male god.

643.   There she sits, all pretty and polished.

644.   No backstory accompanies her as she is there for appearances.

645.   I think we might've gone a bit backwards.

646.   But, frankly, I've noticed that making up deities seems to have become a 'thing'.

647.   Whatever their authenticity or fabrication, the negatives around the female deities have not yet been popularly or convincingly undone, and attempts to do so may still seem a little grasping.

648.   So know this!

649.   *Papa-tua-nuku*, Earth Mother (and Rangi-nui, Sky Father), materialised during the eon of *Te Po*, The Great Darkness. Self-creating. Spontaneous. No magic hand.

650.   The Celestial Grandmothers *Te Whatitiri*, Thunder, resounds and *Te Uira*, Lightning, seeks out.

651.   Without a smidgeon of fragility they call from well above any basement heaven that may have been invented for them.

652.   They crush the idea of passivity and dysfunction.

653.   They tell their own stories from now on.

654.   And so should you.

Insight 34: Uruhia Atua. Imposing Godheads.

655.   I will refrain from imposing a godhead or godheads on you.

656.   Because whether we believe in many deities, a supreme god, a male god, a female god, both or neither,

or no god, there are footsteps in the greater source of our creation—or none.

657.   As you choose.

658.   When we recite *Karakia*, Invocations, or pray, meditate or whatever we do to connect to some greater force, some of us go outwards to our godhead, some go inwards to our unconscious mind, some go elsewhere—some don't care.

659.   We like to belong or to be right or to prove our piety.

660.   We may claim just as vigorously as the next, that our beliefs are truth.

661.   No argument will shift us. Not one.

662.   We may refuse to leave our community, tribe, clan, family, in case we find ourselves on the outside. Alone.

663.   I understand.

664.   I don't seek to validate or discard any of it. It is not my place.

665.   I only seek to share how I understand my old people saw their world.

666.   Take whatever fans your flame—or not.

681.   It is statements of intent, and it creates the necessary conditions for success.

682.   It does not provide for the possibility of failure.

683.   Its language is assertive and commanding.

684.   It is here, now, the eternal present.

685.   Its purpose is to meet any situation with the full capacity to ensure success.

686.   *Karakia* are the monotone chants, using traditional language, symbolism, and structures.

687.   They call upon past events to serve the present.

688.   The intention of the *Tohunga*, Sage, is fixed to and empowered by *Kahukura*, the Collective of *Atua*, the Great Immortals.

689.   His or her *Mana*, prestige, power, and potency, determines how effective their *Karakia* are.

690.   Miracles are for the hopeful ones.

691.   *Karakia* are for the intentional ones.

Insight 36: Whakawhanuitia te Titiro. Look in All Directions.

692.   Some of us are taught to look up to where power is—a legacy of the Missionaries.

693.   One that many of you cherish.

694. So you look up, perhaps to a place where your imagination creates the perfect retirement plan—from our physical existence, that is.

695. Generations of our people now also believe that up is where *Atua*, the Great Immortals, reside.

696. We have adopted the terminology of 'heavens'.

697. But looking up is only part of it.

698. We stand upon the surface of a floating orb.

699. *Whakarongo ki te tangi a te manu e karanga nei.*

700. *Tui, tui, tuituia!*

701. *Tuia i runga, tuia i raro, tuia i roto, tuia i waho.*

702. *Tuia i te here tangata!*

703. Listen to the cry of the bird calling.

704. Bind us, bind us together as one!

705. Bind together that which is above, below, within, and without.

706. Bind together the sacred vine of humankind.

707. We are called together to experience our collective enlightenment and kinship.

708. We are bound to the Infinite Thread and the Sacred Tapestry that connects us all, to us all.

709. Many old *Karakia,* Invocations, reveal there is no supremacy amongst sentient beings, only the

interconnected threads in the fabric upon which we all stand.

710.   The Great Immortals, the rocks, the stars, the tiniest of creatures—and us.

711.   We are all part of the same fabric.

712.   There is no need to bow our heads or direct our *Karakia* upwards.

713.   When we look to the supernatural, the divine, the celestial, or whatever force we choose, it is everywhere.

714.   Close enough to touch.

Insight 37: Tapu. Touched by the Deities.

715.   Those of you who are not from these parts will marvel at the reverence that my people have for this thing we call *Tapu*.

716.   I worry about how on earth you will grasp the idea of it.

717.   So here we go.

718.   Some say *Tapu* is restrictions, sacredness, rules, reverence, danger.

719.   *Tapu* regulates how we access, use, and protect knowledge, the environment, objects, and each other.

720.   Breaching *Tapu* can result in consequences.

721. Some are afraid of this *Tapu*.

722. Some are circumspect.

723. Some are indifferent.

724. First, the source of *Tapu* are *Atua*, Deities, the Great Immortals.

725. *Tapu* is a certain ethereal state characterised by the presence of restrictions with consequences.

726. The wind has *Tapu*. Its source is *Tawhiri-matea*, the Great Immortal of the Many Winds.

727. The crops have *Tapu*. Their source is *Rongo-ma-tane*, the Great Immortal of Cultivated Foods.

728. You have *Tapu*. Its source is *Tu-mata-uenga*, the Great Immortal of War and the Human Condition.

729. Also, we are on the same genetic line as *Papatuanuku*, Earth Mother, and *Ranginui*, Sky Father. They too are the source of our *Tapu*.

730. We have a responsibility to uphold the *Tapu*, the Integrity of the domains of every *Atua*—and ourselves and each other.

731. Our people often try to meet that responsibility.

732. It influences the decisions we make about everything.

733.   It's not always easy. It sometimes requires sacrifice and selflessness.

734.   Second, there are shades and intensities of *Tapu.*

735.   *Tapu* is not a binary state—it is a continuum—affected by conditions and circumstances.

736.   It can be designated, increased or reduced for whatever reason—situation, compromise, convenience, task, state.

737.   We can place ourselves or other things into a state of *Tapu*—and despite information you may have to the contrary, so too can we remove or reduce and return *Tapu* to its source.

738.   When *Tapu* is removed, it is returned to its spiritual origin—the forest, the sky, the ocean, etcetera.

739.   It is an acknowledgement of the assistance given and the instrumental supernatural power for whatever the occasion or task was.

740.   For example, a person becomes *Tapu* when stepping forward to speak on the *marae atea*, the formal Speaking Place of *Tumatauenga*, the Great Immortal Warrior. Their words, therefore, have integrity—well, perhaps not always.

741. Then afterward, the *Tapu* can be reduced to enable them to perform routine things such as mixing and mingling, preparing food, driving home.

742. It is returned to *Tumatauenga*.

743. A new-born baby has full *Tapu* because of their enormous potential—like a tiny spark has the potential to become a roaring inferno.

744. The *Tapu* can be reduced by transgressions, rules broken, adjustments, manipulations, deliberate or not.

745. The *Tapu* of anything may disappear, but it can be activated again.

746. It waxes and wanes.

747. The trick is knowing when and how to reduce or increase *Tapu* as needed.

748. Third, *Tapu* can be restored.

749. Everything has *Tapu*, so when one *Tapu* interacts with another, either a violation or an upholding ensues.

750. A violation may be an act of aggression, damaging another's *Tapu*.

751. A violation may be an act of damaging one's own *Tapu*.

752. An upholding may be an act of kindness, restoring another's *Tapu*.

753.   An upholding may be an act of kindness, restoring one's own *Tapu*.

754.   Restoration is achieved by increasing our Integrity.

755.   O, my head is bursting!

756.   Perhaps I can extract what I believe to be most important.

757.   I believe a true indication of the strength of your *Tapu* is not your ability to violate the *Tapu* of another or of yourself, but to uphold it.

758.   If that is the only thing you take away, then so be it.

Insight 38: Hereheretia te Tapu. Tapu Knots.

759.   Our people are told to adhere to *Tapu* lest some calamity be meted out.

760.   We are in such a state of fear we will surely die of fright!

761.   Fear robs us of our freedom.

762.   And the ability to achieve our purpose is suffocated.

763.   Yet, surely our purpose is why we are here, is it not?

764.   Let us step cautiously towards our emancipation.

765.   The manuscripts show *Tapu* was a functional way to regulate activity and behaviours in ancient times.

766.   It protected food sources, places for rituals, and the integrity of important knowledge, such as genealogies that confirmed and strengthened the survival of our people.

767.   It also protected the *Tohunga*, Sages, who were critical for community wellbeing and such.

768.   The goal was to protect the integrity.

769.   To ensure compliance to *Tapu* rules, a set of dire consequences was communicated to people should they breach them—intentionally or not.

770.   Today, some still like to stoke the fear even when the reason is long forgotten.

771.   Today, some are so enamoured with the idea of *Tapu* they bestow it on everything older than last year's holey socks.

772.   Now we have all sorts of everyday discarded things and knick-knacks upgraded to *Tapu*. Nothing is spared.

773.   They are then carefully guarded, hidden from the general public, placed in a secret drawer or behind a museum's glass display.

774.   Perhaps that is reason enough. Who are we to judge another's allocation of *Tapu* after all?

775.   I am reminded, however, that the source of *Tapu* are *Atua*, Deities, the Great Immortals.

776.   Not everything will deserve such an honourable association.

777.   I suspect we've tied ourselves into *Tapu* knots.

778.   And some of our old people are chuckling from the other side of the shadowy hills.

779.   It is a minefield and everyone has an opinion.

780.   But I will not linger here because our ability to hold to our purpose is of far more interest.

781.   Our task is to disentangle ourselves from our fears and create the conditions necessary to achieve our purpose.

782.   Including how we choose to deal with *Tapu*.

Insight 39: Nga Ture Tapu. Tapu Rules.

783.   Some rules about *Tapu* and when it is activated are still well connected to the original intent—some are not.

784.   A rule with no clue to its reason becomes ritual only—it may have no merit.

Insight 35: Karakia. Invocations.

667.   The *Tohunga*, Sages, were taught to materially create using immaterial means.

668.   Some exceptionally so.

669.   If I may elaborate.

670.   They did not leave all aspects of their lives to chance or to an omnipresent god.

671.   Nor did they hold to the idea that the future was necessarily predetermined, fixed or unchangeable.

672.   Rather, they sought to influence events to their advantage through *Karakia,* Invocations.

673.   An ocean journey, a harvest or a battle were carefully directed.

674.   *Karakia,* Invocations, the art of creation.

675.   *Karakia* does not serve the individual and does not lobby—it leaves that to religion and politics.

676.   Even a *Karakia* that may appear to be for the benefit of a single person is more likely ensuring the individual's contribution to the collective is optimised.

677.   *Karakia* does not plead or bargain.

678.   It is not hopeful.

679.   It does not thank or show gratitude.

680.   It is not recited as a group activity.

785.   The Elders confided, *Tapu* was sometimes used to control others and sometimes the reasons given had no smidgeon of truth.

786.   A tool for manipulation.

787.   We sometimes adhere to what we are instructed about *Tapu* with no clue why.

788.   Some challenge this discretely.

789.   No calamity ensues.

790.   Still. Tread carefully.

791.   Choose what you test and satisfy yourself first.

Insight 40: Mutunga o te Tapu. End of Tapu.

792.   In the manuscripts the *Tohunga*, Sage, writes.

793.   *I kite ano ahau ite mana o nga karakia i mua.*

794.   In former times, he saw the *Mana*, prestige, power, and potency, of the *Karakia*, the Invocations, that were imbued with *Tapu*.

795.   He remembers when his people believed deeply— in their minds and in their hearts.

796.   The old *Tohunga*, Sages, were heartbroken when they realised the *Tapu,* the Influence of *Atua*, the Great Immortals, was over.

797. They said it was when our people turned away to chase the promises of the Colonisers and succumb to the judgement of a new God.

798. The Missionaries redefined *Tapu* and *Karakia* until, in the minds of the people, the 'new *Tapu*', and the 'new *Karakia*' belonged solely to the Colonisers' God.

799. This God hovers above *Te Ira Tangata* and *Te Ira Atua*, the Infinite Thread and the Sacred Tapestry that connects us all, to us all.

800. But he does not occupy it.

801. He does not share his intent.

802. He shakes the threads, and we live or die at his will.

803. When we cast our hopeful prayers to the heavens, we no longer collaborate with *Atua*, the Great Immortals who also stand on threads, all connected, all of the same fabric.

804. The *Tohunga* says when his people accepted this new regime, they suppressed their *Mana* and turned away from the *Tapu*.

805. This is when the sickness commenced, he says.

806. This is when the power of the old *Karakia* ceased.

807.   He says, only when we recognise the *Tapu* of all things—people, creatures, environment, everything—and only when the violations have been put right, only then, will we know a harmonious state.

808.   The *Tohunga* scrawls his final defeatist words on the page.

809.   The *Tapu* is gone.

Insight 41: Te Hononga, Tinana, Wairua. Material, Esoteric Merged.

810.   Humans. Some say we have two parts.

811.   Spirit and body.

812.   Like salt and pepper, bread and cheese, conscious and subconscious.

813.   The *Tupuna*, Ancestors, operated within a system that merged and integrated the esoteric with the material.

814.   Unlike concepts held by, say, religion or science, the *Tohunga*, Sage's, manuscripts show the two worlds were fluid. Constantly.

815.   Sometimes with a flow distinct, sometimes no distinction at all.

816.   When the two share the same current, the tension between dissolves.

817.   To try to detach one from the other was inconceivable.

818.   For many of our people, it is still inconceivable.

Insight 42: Te Ohonga Ake. Awakening.

819.   During the night, we may find ourselves somewhere unfamiliar.

820.   Our dreams have opened a door.

821.   The *Tupuna*, Ancestors, say this is *Te Ohonga*, the Awakening.

822.   How can this be? you ask. How can I be asleep and awake at the same time?

823.   The idea that we go elsewhere during sleep is shared by many cultures.

824.   *Te Ohonga* is where the limitations of our material world no longer restrict us.

825.   Our modern-day perception of time marks out the past, present, and future, but *Te Ohonga* exists in a perpetual now.

826.   An event does not follow the usual rules of 'when'.

827.   Space is disentangled and unravelled, and does not follow the usual rules of 'where'.

828. Archetypical events from the past may be called to the present. Replicated.

829. Scenes may be set. Conditions optimised.

830. Perchance we are confused.

831. Don't worry. We do not need all our questions answered all the time.

832. What matters is what we might gain from *Te Ohonga*.

833. Time, space, and reality are now fluid concepts. Surely anything is possible?

834. To the beginner, the promise of *Te Ohonga* is to fulfil whatever the soaring imagination desires, should he or she learn to wrestle the control of it.

835. The ambitious may harbour lofty desires.

836. But it is like being offered three wishes and completely fumbling the strategy—yes, you might get what you wish for.

837. The humble ones are more easily satisfied with modest yearnings.

838. This night comes so we can visit *Te Ohonga*.

839. Perhaps hold intimate communion with someone who long ago left us for the other side of the shadowy hills.

840.   Someone we once loved, still love.

841.   *Ko te po nei kia moea iho, e awhi reinga ana taua, oho rawa ake nei ki te ao!*

842.   It is where even the simplest want, such as an embrace, can be satisfied.

Insight 43: Ritenga. Ritual.

843.   Some think the *Tohunga*, Sage, uses *ritual* to appease the *Atua*, the old deities, the Great Immortals.

844.   No. *Atua* care not for our quaint and sometimes nonsensical rituals.

845.   Our sacrifices, symbols, and props are what anchor *us* safely to our beliefs.

846.   They help us stay focused, feel vindicated.

847.   The *Atua* are not so petty as to demand rituals before determining whether they will engage with our purpose.

848.   And they are not so easily bribed or entertained.

849.   It is our personal *Mana,* prestige, power, and potency, and the *Mana* of the task they are interested in.

850.   So, do not be afraid to stand one day empty-handed in a paddock with only fenceposts and cow shit.

851.   It is the strength of our *Mana* and intent that determines the outcome, not our ritual props.

Insight 44: Hine-te-iwaiwa. The Great Weaver.

852.   *Hine-te-iwaiwa*, the *Atua*, Great Immortal, responsible for Childbirth.

853.   Some cast her as Midwife, an obligatory respect is given, but modern society tends to undervalue midwives.

854.   It's women's business. Low pay. Poor conditions. All hours. Pulling babies out by the dozens.

855.   *Hine-te-iwaiwa* is also the Great Weaver.

856.   Some cast her as Craftswoman of Cleverly Patterned Mats and Baskets.

857.   Sold at the local market alongside homemade plum jam and organic strawberries.

858.   Perhaps one might purchase a woven article for one's mantlepiece. Or the floor.

859.   We have missed something immensely important.

860.   Why does one *Atua* have two seemingly disparate portfolios?

861.   *Hine-te-iwaiwa* weaves the Infinite Threads that make up the Sacred Tapestry that connects us all, to us all.

862.   Without her we float in a gravity-less space, bump and bounce off each other, drift this way and that, without direction.

863.   *Hine-te-iwaiwa* gently cradles the little one in her arms and shares the pervading breath before placing the child onto its own thread, one of a multitude of strands, all ingeniously connected to each other.

Insight 45: Mauri. Life Force.

864.   How did our old people perceive their connections to everyone and everything?

865.   How did they embody this way of thinking through their actions?

866.   The clue lies in the personified language of the Orators.

867.   *Whakarongo ki te tai o Whatanui e tangi ana*

868.   Listen to the wailing tide of *Whatanui.*

869.   The waves do not just react to the moon's gravitational pull, the inertia or the centrifugal force.

870.   The objectivity of science.

871.   The waves wail.

872.   *Tangi.*

873.   The same word describes the cry of a hungry child or the pain when our lover leaves.

874.   All things have *Ma-uri* or *Mo-uri*.

875.   It is a Consciousness, a Life Essence.

876.   The object, thought or creature is personified.

877.   And our ideas about superiority of so-called living things dissipate.

878.   When an inanimate object is personified, it has a divine right to be tended to.

879.   We have a duty of care because now we are connected to it.

880.   What is there in the world that has no right to be cared for?

881.   Everything has *Ma-uri*.

882.   All of it. All of us.

SECTION 6: LEADERSHIP

Insight 46: Tokotoko. Orator's Ancestral Walking Stick.

883.   Even today, the *Taumata Korero*, Distinguished Orators, flourish their *Tokotoko*, the Orator's Ancestral Walking Stick, on high, as if any account would not be complete without it.

884.   It may be a prop for an old Orator whose knees wobble as he stands to speak, its tip firmly on the floor and its handle gripped tightly.

885.   Or it might be hoisted and twirled theatrically to demonstrate the dexterity of the warrior or the swiftness of the ocean-going vessel.

886.   Oh, even the shaky knees of an old man may not prevent him from hoisting and twirling when the spirit so moves him.

887.   Suddenly, the Orator struts across the floor in the likeness of a bird, and the *Tokotoko* is dramatically thrust to emphasise a pertinent point or, in the least, to gain the attention of those who doze.

888.   Whosoever wields the *Tokotoko* speaks!

889.   The *Tokotoko* is often made especially for the Orator and may have the elaborate, ancient marks of a

carver's hand along its shaft—visual representations of the Orator's lineage and proficiencies.

890.   Let me tell you, a *Tokotoko* can also be other things.

891.   As simple as a twig set upright in a mound of dirt or as impressive as the elongated form of a mystical ocean-going canoe symbolised by a star cluster in the night sky.

892.   The origins of the *Tokotoko* are hidden within the ancient accounts.

893.   In the Creation Story, the Immortal Parents, *Papa-tua-nuku* and *Rangi-nui*, Earth and Sky, are locked in the lovers' embrace.

894.   Their children, who live between them, are forced to creep around in the Great Darkness.

895.   It is not until *Tane*, the Great Immortal of the Forests, forces his parents apart that Light gains entry into the world.

896.   Light that is not of the sun.

897.   Tokona ra, ko Rangi ki runga, ko Papa ki raro. Ka puta mai Te Ao Marama!

898.   *Tane*, this Great Tree, is the *Tokotoko*.

899.   Its real purpose can now be revealed.

900. First, without the *Tokotoko* to hold them separate, *Rangi-nui* and *Papa-tua-nuku* would succumb to their indulgences and return to the embrace.

901. No light—no enlightenment—would penetrate the gloom between.

902. Their children would be crushed again into the Great Darkness.

903. Second, the *Tokotoko* is a channel between the material world and that of the Great Immortals.

904. It is through the *Tokotoko* the intentions of the *Karakia*, the Invocations, are relayed.

905. It is also through the *Tokotoko* that knowledge from the Great Immortals is transmitted to us.

906. The Orator's *Tokotoko* is their conduit to an Enlightened State.

907. They must carry their *Tokotoko* with high regard because they have a duty to only speak the words of *Atua*, the Great Immortals, with the greatest degree of integrity.

Insight 47: Ratonga. Service.

908. The *Karakia*, Invocation, calls upon *Atua*, the Great Immortals, to lend their powers to the matter at hand.

909. Even the Ancient Grandmothers, *Te Whatitiri*, Thunder, and *Te Uira*, Lightning, will respond instantly to the call.

910. It is rare to find a *Tohunga*, Sage, who truly knows how to harness the elements.

911. However, their true goal is not to parade their prowess to an easily impressed audience, but to serve those who depend on them.

912. Leadership is service.

913. Service, not superiority, is their calling.

Insight 48: Ma-rama. Nga Toa. Moon. Warriors.

914. Our *Tupuna*, Ancestors, say it is best the *Toa*, Revered Warrior, dies when the moon is at its brightest.

915. When *Te Ma-Rama*, The Celestial Lamp discharges its dazzling light.

916. So the sacred pathway can be clearly seen.

917. Better to die in the phase of the full moon, *Te Rakau-nui*, than when it wanes.

918.   When both man and moon wither in the darkness.

919.   But the skirmishes of former times are gone.

920.   Warriors no longer die courageously by the strike of an enemy's weapon.

921.   He longs for a great war, so he might make a final display.

922.   Instead, the *Toa* dies in the faint light of his old age.

923.   The darkened moon barely illuminates his weapon—once swung with might in defence of his people—and now fallen from his furrowed hand.

924.   It is difficult to know how to honour a death when it arrives in the comfort of an old man's bed.

925.   Who will lead us into the fray and who will cast light upon the sacred pathway now both the warrior and the winter moon are extinguished?

926.   E ui ana koe, kei hea te marama? He Tangaroa-a-mua. He paunga korekore.

927.   You ask, what phase is it of the moon?

928.   It is *Tangaroa-o-mua*, the last quarter.

929.   It is the cusp of *Te Korekore*, the moon that will soon be no more than a shadow.

930.　We should not mourn bygone days of warriors, battles, and full moons.

931.　*Ka hutia te tohunga ki runga ki a Rona.*

932.　Instead, we shall hoist this warrior on high where he shall reside with the waxing moon where *Rona*, the Controller of the Tides, awaits.

Insight 49: Rangatira. Leaders.

933.　There are those rare individuals whom we consider *Rangatira*, Weavers of People, Leaders.

934.　They do not self-proclaim or hunger for recognition or glory.

935.　They do not strive for our survival, for that alone has no meaning.

936.　They strive to elevate us all, so we are worthy of survival.

937.　When the *Tupuna*, Ancients, acknowledge these *Rangatira*, they do so metaphorically and with eloquence.

938.　*Taku ate hoki ra, taku rata tu tahi, taku whakamarumaru.*

939.　*Unuhia atu ra te taniwha ite rua.*

940.　*Hare ra o nui, o maru.*

941.　*E kore e arumia i muri i to tua i nga mana.*

942.   Ko wai i tohu ai, e hoea te moana?

943.   Ka pai ra pea, ka pakuu to toki kite waka ka rangona e te iwi.

944.   O, my heart, my solitary rata tree, my shelter.

945.   The illustrious creature has now withdrawn from its lair.

946.   I farewell your greatness.

947.   There will be no other who will follow, for the urge expires with you.

948.   Who will foretell whether these ardent seas will once again be crossed?

949.   It is, perhaps, sufficient that your axe-blow resounded upon the canoe and was heard by all.

SECTION 7: WHO WE ARE

Insight 50: Ko Wai Koe! Who Are You! The Outlier.

950.   Our people can be sceptical and judgemental.

951.   It is one of our less-endearing characteristics.

952.   No wonder suspicion visits.

953.   Especially if one is not chosen, has no mandate, and possesses unverifiable or conflicting information.

954.   The Outlier enjoys the freedom the position offers because no-one can contain him or her or you.

955.   Not even when the Interrogators demand, *Ko wai koe!* Who are you!

956.   Perhaps they should direct their question to the whispering rafters.

957.   Where the voice of the *Whaea*, Matriarch, replies to their question with another.

958.   She tosses it back to the Interrogator. *Ko wai koe!*

Insight 51: Te Tini Me Te Mano. Multitude.

959.   Our *Tupuna*, Ancestors, spoke of *Te Tini Me Te Mano*, the Multitude, the extended family, all of humanity.

960.   In its broadest definition, the Multitudes comprise *Atua,* the Great Immortals, the Deities, our Ancestors and loved ones who gather on the other side of the shadowy hills, and those of us who still walk this Earth.

961.   Oh yes, we are connected to the many *Atua* through unbroken genealogical, cosmogenic bloodlines!

962.   They say they create and orchestrate everything.

963.   But they are us through bloodlines, and humans can influence them due to the pervading connection of all things.

964.   Some humans are very good at it. We call them *Tohunga,* Sages.

965.   We are amongst *Te Tini Me Te Mano,* the Multitudes.

966.   We are not alone.

967.   So when we wish to call upon all of them, all of us, the most powerful of them, to fulfil some important task, we should not hesitate.

Insight 52: Ko Wai Ahau. Who Am I.

968.   *Ko wai ahau!* Who am I!

969.   It is not a question. It is a demand waiting for an answer.

970. Stop what you are doing for a moment.

971. Identify yourself. *Ko wai ahau!*

972. Who are we when stripped of our acquired things?

973. That is, when we have no possessions requiring us to hold jobs, jobs for money, money for jam, jam for toast, toast and egos.

974. Let us unmask ourselves and let go our fantasies.

975. Then we are open to accept other fantasies, whether or not we are cast in the role of hero.

976. Who are we when we are not laden?

977. When we find the answer, perhaps we will decide to plug ourselves back into the grid, *Te Ira Tangata*, the Infinite Thread that connects us all, to us all.

978. For today, we are disconnected, addicted to acquisitions, group mentalities, and entitlements.

979. We have traded our responsibilities for what we believe are necessary memberships to higher orders—our religions, our gods, our governments, our careers, and our status.

980. In doing so, we have unwittingly become part of a mass disconnection where humans wreak havoc upon each other and the world.

981.   The realisation of who we are and our relationship with *Te Ira Tangata* is a revolution against individualism and selfishness.

982.   We are not just the oppressor, the exploiter or the enemy.

983.   Nor are we the target, the victim or the casualty.

984.   Again.

985.   *Ko wai ahau?* Who am I?

986.   I inhale the same air you exhale, and you, mine.

987.   Ko A-Hau.

988.   I am the pervading breath that is yours and mine.

989.   I am the vital essence that is yours and mine.

990.   I am the life force that is yours and mine.

991.   Time to plug back in.

Insight 53: He Tatai. Ancestral Lineage.

992.   *He Tatai*, the Ancestral Lineage, is passed down by the old Sages to subsequent Knowledge-Keepers.

993.   The Lineage identifies our placement on the Infinite Genetic Thread.

994.   It literally links us to our *Tupuna*, Ancestors— name by name by name.

995. Let us start at the beginning, for then we will see where we come from.

996. The lineage begins with *Atua*, the Great Immortals, the Deities, the original parents, *Rangi-nui*, Sky Father, and *Papa-tua-nuku*, Earth Mother.

997. It continues to their deity children and grandchildren.

998. And onwards, until eventually it reaches those who evolve from deity to human, our ancestors. The progeny.

999. It goes on and on for what seems like eternity, until eventually it reaches the name we've been waiting for.

1000. Ours.

1001. We may puff out our chest and exclaim, *Oh yes, I am genealogically connected to the Gods no less!*

1002. Indeed.

1003. However, the old people never swaggered and pranced about so.

1004. On *Te Ira Tangata* and *Te Ira Atua*, the Infinite Threads, we have no need to be enamoured by our fancy connections or our resulting brilliance by association.

1005. That would feed a delusion that we are somehow superior because we are in the likeness of, or from, a superior *Atua* or god.

1006. This belief has us discarding our direct responsibility to everything.

1007. We permit our superior god-like self to ride roughshod over the planet, people, and creatures, to exploit, misuse, and discard.

1008. This is not the way of our old people and does not come from the knowledge embedded in our Ancestral Lineage.

1009. Our connection to the Great Immortals is not so we can adorn our topknot.

1010. It is so we can serve their purpose to our Kin.

1011. Step back onto *Te Ira Tangata* and *Te Ira Atua*, the Infinite Threads.

1012. Look around, everywhere, into the distance, every direction.

1013. There we cannot live in the deception of our own brilliance.

1014. Instead, can we not see the true brilliance of everything?

1015. Ka rikoriko mai koe i Te Ira Tangata.

1016. You are a tiny iridescent glowing amongst infinitesimal glowings.

1017. Yes, *Te tini me te mano*, the Multitudes.

1018. Accept this instead.

1019. And believe me when I tell you it is only there, you glisten flawlessly.

Insight 54: Ehara Ko Au. Cult of Other.

1020. The Cult of Other is where anything not of us, falls outside our genuine consideration.

1021. *Othering* allows us to provide for our own needs ahead of everyone and everything else.

1022. It is a creation in our mind to establish an unequal relationship based on domination and subordination.

1023. It comes from the worldviews of *Nga Tangata Matapiko*, the Empire-Builders.

1024. It helps us detach from the horrors in the news.

1025. It helps us believe we can do nothing, or we don't have to.

1026. It helps us rest our heads peacefully on our pillows each night.

1027. The Othering goes further.

1028. We deem a rock to be an inanimate object, the winds to be a scientific phenomenon, and the universe to be a mathematical calculation.

1029. In relegating almost everything to Other we feel justified in discarding, exploiting, and abusing.

1030. There is no empathy, no responsibility, no desire to act sustainably or to think about cycles and systems.

1031. This is our individual undoing—and by extension, the undoing of all of us.

1032. The Infinite Threads, *Te Ira Atua, Te Ira Tangata*, and our unison with each other, the animals, stars, rocks, rivers, forests, and mountains, connects us all, to us all.

1033. If we do not honour all of it, all of us, we are headed down a treacherous path.

1034. This is not some quaint Indigenous philosophy we can cherry-pick from.

1035. This is our survival.

Insight 55: Nga Kaute. Numbers.

1036. From the beginning we are poked, prodded, and measured to satisfy a contrived mathematical measurement of us.

1037. We are someone's calculation.

1038. Our estimated conception date (a) plus 280 gestation days (b) equals the day of our expected birth (x).

1039. So a + b = x with an acceptable relative margin of error, that is, the result of a percentage of confidence (z) times the square root of the proportion (p) times (1 - p) over the sample size (n).

1040. Yet 95 percent of us were not born on the date known as x.

1041. Once our foetal form becomes quantifiable, our dimensions are sized up and jotted down for comparative analysis.

1042. Our appendages are counted—five of this, five of that, one of those, so many heart beats per minute, *te mea, te mea,* etcetera, etcetera.

1043. From the comfort of our tiny womb universe through to and beyond our expulsion into daylight, we are carefully socialised.

1044. Soon, we are an obedient little soldier shuffling through life according to the time pieces and cartographic representations of modern society. The numbers.

1045. We are encouraged to obsess over our salary, our bank account, our lateness, our punctuality, our age, our weight, the circumference of our flexed bicep or dainty waist, the latitudes and longitudes, the arrivals and the returns, the whens and wheres.

1046. We are so fixated on these numbers, we fail to notice the ebb and flow, the wax and wane, the dawn and dusk, and the slow trajectory of orbs through the night sky.

1047. When we are asked for our numbers upon meeting a stranger, we may recognise another of our fellow soldiers, for they are everywhere.

1048. Our worth is measured not by numbers, but by *Te Hononga,* Connections, Relationships.

1049. When our people greet you with, *Tena koe,* they are saying, there you are in my presence, and I in yours. I respectfully acknowledge you because you and I both occupy *Te Ira Tangata,* the Infinite Genetic Thread.

1050. When our people ask, *No hea koe?,* Where are you from?, they wish to identify your common genealogical connections through 'place'.

1051. They ask, who is the mountain you love so well, so I may, perchance, ascertain my mountain's connection to yours?

1052. Oh, you are of the sea people, or the bush people or the river or snow people.

1053. Where are the remnants of your Ancestors' bones?

1054. From where does your blood flow, so I may know if my blood flows alongside?

1055. When they ask your name—*Ko wai to ingoa?*— they wish to establish the finer points of your ancestral connections.

1056. They inquire not only after your name, but those of your Grandparents, so they may discover the genealogical convergences between you, however distant.

1057. Why do our people do this?

1058. Because they hope to finally, and in all knowingness, share the breath of life with you—as Kin.

Insight 56: Tu-mata-uenga. To Tatou Kaitiaki. Our Protector.

1059. The primal parents, *Rangi-nui,* Sky Father, and *Papa-tua-nuku,* Earth Mother, were prised from the lover's embrace.

1070. Even the promise of an afterlife does not convince us to release our grip.

1071. We constantly glance back because *Te Hemonga*, Death, is at our heels.

1072. Oh, time is short and we must hurry because death is the only certainty.

1073. We are persuaded our life's goal is to hastily elevate ourselves to some self-seeking triumph before we expire.

1074. To seize what we want.

1075. Put a longer list into the bucket.

1076. In case we miss out.

1077. In case we are forgotten.

1078. To leave footprints everywhere, with little regard.

1079. Someone else will clean up after us.

1080. *Te Hemonga* remains abstract in our minds, until one day it forces us to see, *Kanohi-ki-te-kanohi*, face to face, eye to eye.

1081. The fabric has ruptured, and something close to the bone is calling us in.

1082. Our most intimate relationship with death is also our most intimate relationship with our Kinship.

1083. We cast our dead to Earth or Sky.

1084. It is only right that we return to the fold of our *Whanaungatanga*—Kinship with everything.

1085. Dust. Ash. Smoke. Earth. Renewal.

SECTION 8: HUMAN NATURE

Insight 58: Kia Ora Ake te Hau. Good Health.

1086. I do not tread softly as if you possess not an ounce of courage.

1087. The information relating to our health has been perilously displaced.

1088. Society encourages an extraordinarily distorted sense of entitlement and self-destruction

1089. Dangling treats, vices, excuses, and idleness before us.

1090. We are determined to be led by *Te Ihu,* the Sacred Nose, to some no-good destination.

1091. We only remember our mortality when the consequence of exercising our rights is our ill health.

1092. Then we claim helplessness, seek sympathy, and demand medical attention from a system that profits from our demise.

1093. We design a future of anguish for our loved ones who may care for us in our deterioration.

1094. They sacrifice their needs for ours, and eventually they grieve.

1095. We are willing consumers of things that cause ailments to our bodies.

1096. We are enamoured with the moments of joy they promise.

1097. Even when knowing that our destructive habits will result in our downfall.

1098. We'll worry about it later. When it's too late.

1099. Each to their own.

1100. Our *Tupuna*, Ancestors, strove to contribute productively to the community.

1101. To not do so would cause shame they could not bear.

1102. And consequences.

1103. We cannot change our past decisions.

1104. But let us raise the hand of silence against our future excuses.

1105. We still have the *right* to contribute to our family and our people—and the *will* to do so as fully as we can.

Insight 59: Whakahihi. Mahaki. Arrogance. Humility

1106. Some of us believe we are superior.

1107. We deduce that all we see below us is less.

1108. This belief has us discarding our responsibilities every day.

1109. It is not my fault, we say. There is nothing I can do. Surely you cannot expect me to fix this. They brought it upon themselves. It is the way of the world. Fate and destiny. The will of a higher power. Let me get back to numbing my mind with reality tee vee.

1110. So, we permit our superior self to ride roughshod over the planet and our Kin.

1111. Believing that the responsibility for the pain we cause, is not ours to answer.

1112. Believing that the responsibility for the pain others cause, is not ours to put right.

1113. We cannot. We will not.

1114. For it is surely part of a much bigger purpose, and we are not privy to it.

1115. It is time for us to abandon this fiction.

1116. *Whakahihi,* Arrogance, is not an endearing trait.

1117. The ancient *Karakia,* Invocation, tells us to stand down.

1118. Our old people struggled with the idea of *Whakahihi*—Arrogance, because it is a trait belonging to an individualistic worldview and is in opposition to a culture that values collective well-being and success.

1119. *Mahaki*, Humility, is the opposite. It does not seek to be front and centre. It better serves the collective.

1120. Today, here and now in this colonised reality, we straddle two opposing worldviews.

1121. One expects humility, or risk being knocked down by our own; the other applauds self-promotion, or risk being left out.

1122. No wonder we have so many humble-braggers trying hard to serve both worlds.

1123. Stumbling along the fine line between the two.

1124. The delusion of our self-importance collapses when the *Karakia* affirms we are in the presence of powerful forces—*Papatuanuku*, Earth, *Ranginui*, Sky, *Te Whatitiri*, Thunder, *Te Uira*, Lightning, *Tanemahuta*, Forests, and *Tangaroa*, Oceans.

1125. Our most important revelation will arrive when our over-zealous sense of superiority is shattered, and we are left with raw humility—not one we feel the need to announce, but one that leaves us speechless.

1126. Only then can we look without the blindness of arrogance and see we are one of *Te Tini me te Mano*, the countless Multitudes.

1127. And that will be more than enough.

Insight 60: Makutu. Curse.

1128. *Kai kinikini ai te mamae i ahau e, koi noho au i te ao taha maero ai e, hirihiritia ra, e hika, to takiri e.*

1129. If my pain within gnaws and I dwell in a drifting listlessness, then, my dear friend, will you chant a spell to allay my twitching, my omen?

1130. You may have heard talk of *Makutu*, the casting of spells to inflict harm.

1131. It is whispered that *Makutu* is the reason for the chaos and disturbance in our bodies and minds. And some might say, our world.

1132. We conclude someone has cursed us.

1133. We look no further into this demise because we have now discovered the cause for sure, and have decided we can do nothing to remedy it.

1134. We mock the idea that one's belief may manifest as physical ill health or bad luck.

1135. Yet, we accept the mind's ability to heal medical conditions using the placebo effect, or to create illness using the nocebo effect, after all it is well documented in medical circles.

1136. Let us agree this is about what is occupying the mind.

1137. The *Tupuna*, Ancestors, believed illness could be brought about by the focused intentions of a third party.

1138. They also believed it could be countered.

1139. Thus, *Makutu* equally inflicts or deflects harm.

1140. One would hurl harm towards another in a malicious or revengeful act.

1141. The other would hurl it back in equal if not more damaging measure.

1142. The inevitable outcome of all of this *hurling* could be the death of one or the other, and the possible ongoing repercussions upon the loser's descendants.

1143. Oh yes, the demolition of *Makutu* can be visited upon generations.

1144. When we are at a loss, *Makutu* suffices as an explanation.

1145. It is easy for us to say, *It must be the curse!*

1146. Even when the offence has long been forgotten.

1147. Our helplessness brings us to despair, and we resign to our fate.

1148. But our defeatism only shows we have failed to challenge our beliefs.

1149. The *Tupuna*, Ancestors, did not just accept their fate. They challenged it.

1060. Their sons no longer wished to dwell in darkness between the two.

1061. They desired their parents' separation so that *Maramatanga*, Light's Illumination, could be cast into the space between Earth and Sky.

1062. However, the one faithful son, *Tawhiri-matea*, the Great Immortal of the Many Winds, was angered by the disloyalty shown by his brothers.

1063. The separation was successful, light came, and *Tawhiri-matea* pledged revenge unending.

1064. His deluge is unleashed even today.

1065. Howling gales and fierce squalls are repeatedly hurled upon his siblings.

1066. It is only his brother *Tu-mata-uenga*, the Great Immortal of War and the Human Condition, who battles against this torrent.

1067. He seeks to protect *Te Ira Tangata*, the Infinite Genetic Thread—us.

1068. It is *Tu-mata-uenga* who is also called when *Te Hemonga*, Death, steps upon our pathway.

Insight 57: Te Hemonga. Death.

1069. We are concerned with preserving our mortality.

1150. Well, some did. Some simply succumbed.

1151. A *Tohunga*, Sage, of great *Mana*—prestige, power and potency, was duly commissioned to perform an ancient *Karakia*, Invocation, to bring the sorry situation to an end.

1152. Specifically, she or he would harness *Atua*, the Great Immortals, for their influential powers.

1153. The *Karakia* would be recited with confidence and strength, for a trembling voice and shaking knees is a sign of doubt—an insult to the *Atua* concerned.

1154. Still, let us not assume *Atua* would take up the cause of a mere mortal on some mission—unless it aligned with theirs.

1155. Indifference was a possibility. They are not at our beck and call, and do not suffer fools.

1156. The success of the *Karakia* was also linked to the size of the *Mana* of said *Tohunga*.

1157. Should the mission strike the fancy of an *Atua*, and the *Mana* of the *Tohunga* be of a sufficient size, then the *Atua* would help her or him to reveal the source of the chaos, suppress it, announce the situation resolved, and safeguard against future harm.

1158. Of course, the same *Karakia* performed by a *Tohunga* of inferior *Mana* would have no effect at all.

1159. Underlying success is an unswerving belief.

1160. Belief has power. Fear has no place. Discard it.

1161. Replace fear with fortitude.

1162. The *Atua* will be on side.

Insight 61: Kaingaki Mara. Rangimarie. Gardeners. Peace.

1163. The old manuscripts tell of two kinds of warriors.

1164. The first is *Te Toa Taua*, the Skilful Adept of War who is in constant danger.

1165. When these warriors fail, they are slain, and another must take their place.

1166. All that accumulated skill, gone, in one distracted moment.

1167. Today, many leaders focus on military and commercial enterprise.

1168. Both take land and resources for plunder, and justify their endless means.

1169. Their warriors toil under the mantle of *Tu-mata-uenga*, the Great Immortal of War and the Human Condition.

1170. The hostilities of those who return from the battlefields come to an end under *Rongo-ma-tane*, the Great Immortal of Peaceful Endeavours and Cultivated Food.

1171. What is this strange juxtaposition of Peace and Cultivation brought by *Rongo-ma-tane*?

1172. *Te Ahi Kaa*, the Keepers of the Home Fires, know it is not proper to take land and squander it.

1173. We do not truly occupy it unless we *keep it warm*.

1174. This is the undertaking of *Te Toa Ngaki Kai*, the Skilful Adept of Food Cultivation.

1175. Yes. The second warrior is the Gardener.

1176. If *Te Toa Taua*, constantly at war, fails, he or she will be gone. Another must take their place.

1177. But if the Gardener fails, what of it?

1178. Gardeners live to try again and again until they become adept.

1179. When cultivations have more status than war and financial enterprise, it will be the Gardener who leads us.

1180. Through cultivation he or she will toil under the mantle of *Rongo-ma-tane* and show hospitality and generosity in the sharing of the harvest.

1181. There will always be those who would rather raid the crops of others than grow their own.

1182. However, when we are all tending our gardens, when all are fed and all are engaged productively, the need to take up arms is quelled and the realisation of Peace is affirmed.

Insight 62: Tangata Matapiko. Mean People.

1183. In this world of disarray all has been shredded.

1184. Now there are only bones and entrails.

1185. The Elders pull remnants of wool from their eyes.

1186. They lament, for they were so easily tricked into robbing their *Tama-ariki*, Revered Children, of their legacy.

1187. In a crisis some bring their best. Some bring their worst.

1188. The pendulum swings wide.

1189. The people ready themselves for rebellion.

1190. *Tangata Matapiko,* the Insatiable Ones, doers of deeds most foul, manipulators of the masses, snigger behind their iron gates—tossing bloody scraps over the fences.

1191. Our youngsters survey the damage and wonder how they will stop the stinging ocean spray that blows ferociously over stripped lands.

1192. *E tama! E tangi. He moho tangata, he whenua mehameha. Puputai e wawa whenua.*

1193. *Whakau e tama! Nga hau o te uru, ko Ngungunu, ko Ngangana, me ko Aparangi.*

1194. O Child, lamenting. They are treacherous people, and now the land is desolate. The sea spray spews over the empty land.

1195. Stand fast, Child, the winds of the west are cyclonic, tempestuous, and long prevailing.

Insight 63: Huatau. Grace.

1196. Amidst this madness you ask about Grace.

1197. Grace makes no effort to be revealed.

1198. It is simplicity. It is meticulous. It is profound.

1199. It is the calm exterior from afar and the unexpected detail up close.

1200. Grace is found even when facing the final conflict.

1201. Grace is not in the perfect execution of your weaponry skills, but in how you seek to avoid the demolition of battle.

1202. It is not in the accumulation of abundance, but in your poise amidst poverty.

1203. It is not in your search for crowds to follow, so you can avoid loneliness, but in the dignity of your solitude.

1204. Grace is the way you uphold your authenticity, even when your identity has been torn asunder.

1205. I cannot tell you where your path will lead amidst this chaos.

1206. But you have asked about Grace.

1207. I can only say you will find it when your stride is determined, your gaze is concentrated, and your movement is illuminated.

1208. *Ka nui o whakaaro atawhai ina puaki o mangai.*

1209. Grace will be present when your voice utters only wisdom against the adversity that lies ahead.

Insight 64: Kore Tuhononga. Disconnection.

1210. Our darkest fears do not come in the form of a bogeyman hiding under the bed.

1211. Our darkest fears are aloneness, exclusion, banishment.

1212. Disconnection.

1213. That is why we follow our flock. Our tribe. Our people.

1214. Even when the flock wanders into absurdity.

Insight 65: Aroha Whakaingoingo. Romantic Love.

1215. Let me lay down the enchanting words of romance once spoken by our old people—musings for your heart.

1216. No doubt, I will fail to convey the aspirations of the ancient Lover due in part to the inadequacy of the language we now converse in.

1217. Still. Humour me.

1218. For in this ancient time, love is not brought upon the scented petals of freshly plucked flowers, nor is it concealed inside ornamented boxes loosely ribboned and bowed.

1219. It drifts upon the gentle breeze and passes above the bubbling waters of the Wellspring-of-Tender-Intent.

1220. What is this delicate wind that touches your skin?

1221. Perhaps you do not yearn for my love, and yet …

1222. There, the breeze settles softly by your side.

1223. A companion to our repose.

1224. It is Effervescence from Love's Wellspring.

1225. *Pupu ake-a-wai to aroha.*

Insight 66: Mahi Ngatahi. Whakataetae. Cooperation. Competition.

1226. Ancient Navigators *Nukutawhiti* and *Ruanui* arrived from the mystical island homelands of Hawaiki to the spectacular Hokianga Harbour, in the Southern Pacific Ocean.

1227. They voyaged on separate vessels and defeated overwhelming obstacles in the spirit of cooperation.

1228. Upon arrival, each sought to build a *Whare Wananga*, House of Esoteric Knowledge, on either side of the Hokianga Harbour.

1229. Each man promised they would celebrate their House openings together.

1230. The promise was broken.

1231. *Ruanui* sought to open earlier.

1232. The phrase *Hokianga Whakapau Karakia*, Hokianga of Depleted Invocations, signals an unfortunate shift in their relationship.

1233. The two men pitted themselves against each other.

1234. The Houses and people were forgotten, as each determined to outwit the other.

1235. They competed to the probable annoyance of a *Tohoraha*, Whale—who was, by all accounts, to be called forth to provide food for the first opening event.

1236. None of us like to be used.

1237. While one man invoked the whale's arrival, the other sent it back out to sea.

1238. They repeated this inane act over and over until they ran out of invocations.

1239. Then, their competitiveness escalated into hostility.

1240. Death ensued.

1241. Now, *Nukutawhiti* was eliminated, *Ruanui* and his people left the *Hokianga* forever.

1242. It was a great loss to all.

1243. To what end?

1244. Unless war is afoot, and division and chaos is a purpose, competition has little place. Even in war and chaos, it likely has little place.

1245. Competition is self-serving and fails humanity and the earth.

1246. Nowhere in the many manuscript accounts about *Tohunga*, Knowledge-Keepers, does it say their accomplishments are achieved by competition.

1247. Should they not strive only to serve and carry their people forward—not to flaunt and receive trinkets as proof of their prowess?

1248. Yet, we boast of our Sages, Orators, and Philosophers.

1249. Challenge others to present their equals for inspection.

1250. Indulge in gratuitous intellectual and spiritual excess.

1251. Showing off.

1252. It is of no value to do so.

1253. And our old people would say, we will never reach our full potential.

Insight 67: Tohu. Nga Hiahia. Signs. Desire.

1254. *Tohu*, Signs, can be easily misread in favour of one's desires.

1255. We must learn to check when the ache to have our desires met overwhelms us—then suddenly we see *Tohu* everywhere.

1256. Surely the signs will confirm what we already knew—so we tell ourselves.

1257. The role of our physical self is to observe the *Tohu*.

1258. The role of our intellectual self is to filter out delusion.

1259. The role of our spiritual self is to deeply understand its significance.

1260. Engage all three when dealing with *Tohu*.

Insight 68: Na Wai Te He. Blame.

1261. Blame.

1262. A deliberate act whereby we escape responsibility for our circumstances.

1263. We are the defender of our positions, the protector of our beliefs, the preserver of our egos, the blockages to our progress—and the diluter of our *Mana*, our prestige, power, and potency.

1264. We are consumed by blame.

1265. Our dedication to it is more important than finding ways to put things right.

1266. We aim to induce guilt.

1267. We demonise our perpetrators and all of their kind.

1268. We crave a reaction.

1269. We corner our audience.

1270. See? They did this, and they did that!

1271. Yes, they did. Still. Put away your pointing finger.

1272. We are talking about you, not them.

1273. Of course, fair blame and reparation are right and proper.

1274. However, are we blind to the subtleties of our responsibilities?

1275. Consider that today each of our decisions will contribute to our situation.

1276. Let us accept some blame even if it is for when we last wasted precious time whinging.

1277. We still protest. We say if we accept even the smallest amount of blame, then the perpetrators' liability will be reduced because they will not take responsibility.

1278. They will gloat.

1279. They will still resent us.

1280. They will still have contempt for our inability to pick ourselves up and for focusing on them instead of our solution.

1281. We so clearly demonstrate our weakness.

1282. Perchance we see nothing beyond blame?

1283. Let us quell all of it.

1284. This ceaseless blaming has left us jaded.

1285. We secretly think it now defines us.

1286. Perhaps it is time to understand the nature of our *Mana.*

1287. Ask, who am I? Why do I do what I do? Where is my integrity? How do I determine the worth of my actions? Am I powerless? Am I powerful? Am I aligned with my beliefs?

1288. When we let go our attachment to blame, we mark out a new trail.

1289. Fortified. Resilient. Determined.

1290. *He toka tumoana, ka tu, ka tu, ka tu.*

1291. *Ahakoa i awhatia mai te rangi, whakapakakatia ite whitinga o te ra, te toka tumoana, ka tu, ka tu, ka tu!*

1292. The rock stands resolutely in the sea, no matter the raging storms, the crashing waves, and the burning sun.

1293. Fault and blame come and go, and the rock endures in the midst of it all.

Insight 69: Whakaepaepa. Indulgence.

1294. We are a generation that has come to expect reward with little effort.

1295. We are selectively ignorant of the impact our reward-seeking has on the suffering of others.

1296. We convince ourselves that our luxuries are a birthright and are the basic necessities of our privileged lives.

1297. Our distance from reality is not entirely our fault.

1298. We are the much loved *Mokopuna*, Grandchildren, of a generation that suffered the unspeakable when a foreign invasion, an epidemic, two world wars, and a depression all occurred within a single lifespan.

1299. They were determined their children and grandchildren should never know such horrors.

1300. So they substituted indulgence for scarcity.

1301. Unintentionally, they assisted in the rise of unprecedented exploitation.

1302. Today, the two extremes of suffering and indulgence have been met.

1303. The divide between them is great.

1304. An indicator of civilisation—or lack of it.

1305. Our continued ignorance, however, is no longer tolerable.

1306. Even you must know this.

1307. It is time to re-balance. It is time for restraint. It is time for productivity.

1308. It is time to appreciate simple rewards that do no harm.

1309. Who will teach us this?

1310. The *Tupuna*, Ancestors, say it is *Tatarakihi*, Cicada.

1311. He does so with the beauty and grace of an Elder.

1312. He is the Bird of Sirius; *Ko te Manu o Rehua*, the Immortal who presides over Midsummer and the star Sirius in the constellation of Canis Major.

1313. *Tatarakihi* emerges from the warmth of *Papa-tua-nuku*, Earth Mother, after a diligent winter, to herald the summer.

1314. His muscles rapidly buckle in and out of his hollow abdomen, amplifying the resonance and enabling us, along with the object of his desire, to hear his *Waiata*, his Chorus.

1315. Who else but *Tatarakihi* understands the true and simple delight of basking on a tree after a long winter of prudence and industry?

1316. Who else will sing the song of summer with such purity and sweetness?

1317. The Old Man writes.

1318. U mai tatou ki te keri i te rua, mo te ua o te rangi mo te makariri wero i te Po nei, me te kohi mai ano i te kakano hei o ake ma tama-roto, kia ora ai.

1319. He pai aha koia taaku, he noho noa, piri ake ki te peka o te rakau. Ina, ina, noa ake ki te Ra e whiti nei, me te whakatangi kau i aku paihau. Ta-ra-ra-ta, ki-ta, ki-ta, wiri o papa, to-ene, to-ene!

1320. He translates: Come hither and together let us bore a pit to shield from rains, which pour from wintry skies with chilling blast. Here collect the seed, which shall our inner-selves sustain.

1321. What is my chief, nay, sole delight? To cling me close to the branch of the tree and to bask in sunshine warm and bright, and rustle these my wings with glee. O, quivering sides, sound your refrain!

Insight 70: Mataku. Fear.

1322. We ask our Knowledge-Keepers about the secret esoteric knowledge of the Ancients, particularly *Wairua* things.

1323. Some may call it Spiritual Essence, some may call it Sacred.

1324. We are told of the *Tapu*, things under the influence of *Atua*, the Great Immortals, and are told we should not dabble.

1325. We pursue our query and are told we do not have the right, are not chosen, cannot handle it, and so on.

1326. We are advised not to pester for answers, but we do anyway.

1327. Finally, we are fairly warned, it is not safe.

1328. And cautioned against provoking unwanted repercussions.

1329. Death is proposed as a real possibility.

1330. Now we are petrified, we moderate our aspirations within the acceptable confines of our fear.

1331. We concede that fear is part of our cultural belief system and compliance is virtuous—we only wish to belong, after all.

1332. Fear leads to mediocrity.

1333. We cannot achieve magnificence if fear is our companion.

1334. We have been misinformed.

1335. *Tapu* is not fear. They are two different things.

1336. The fear-monger knows all about control and oppression.

1337. It is attractive to those who gain from sustaining it in others.

1338. While fear grips us, we will not meddle where they do not want us.

1339. It is offered by those who do not want our elevated consciousness to unleash a defiant, self-determined, and independent warrior.

1340. We can give them their wish, or we can take our freedom.

1341. We ask, who told us about this fear? Who told them? What was the motive? Is this fear real or contrived?

1342. If we could whisper what we believe about this fear in our heart—where none will see and none will judge—what would we say?

1343. The journey to *Te Ao Marama*, the Enlightenment, is one that requires us to free ourselves from fear.

1344. They do not travel together.

1345. The bird tries to flutter away but is ensnared in the bushes.

1346. *Me he manu motu ite mahanga.*

1347. We are the bird that has escaped the snare.

1348. Only if we are free from fear, can we fly above the leafy canopy into the brightness.

1349. There, clarity is found.

1350. We will not find it if we are still trapped in the foliage.

Insight 71: Waiata Aroha. Songs of Sorrow and Joy.

1351. The old manuscripts contain many *Waiata Aroha.*

1352. They have a narrow band of melody, sung in chant style like no other you have heard.

1353. They are heart-driven pulses, elusive rhythms.

1354. In our culture, there are times when our emotions cannot be expressed as tears.

1355. So, we find resilience in song.

1356. *Kahore te aroha e huri i runga ra.*

1357. Your yearning overwhelms you.

1358. At first, the words appear to speak of love, yet they seem devastatingly sad.

1359. Why do sorrow and joy share the same melodious expression?

1360. We are misled when the word love along with its Western cultural context is substituted for the word *Aroha*.

1361. *Te Aro*, the Presence of, *Te Ha*, the Pervading Breath that imbues all things, all time, all space.

1362. *Te Ha* is the gasp, the exhalation, the deep inflow, and the hearty expulsion.

1363. You cannot follow it with your eyes.

1364. It is indiscernible. It is uplifting. It is the life force.

1365. *Aroha* seeks the bounty in all things.

1366. *Aroha* seeks *Whanaungatanga*—the Kinship of all things.

1367. *Aroha* manifests as the deep affection that accompanies the essence of Kinship, its delight and its grief.

1368. So, now you know.

1369. There is no void between sorrow and joy.

1370. They both alight on love's stage.

Insight 72: Putanga Mai o te Riri. Anger. Violence.

1371. Anger and violence.

1372. It is the most challenging thing to draw upon my compassion when so much violence goes unchecked.

1373. We lose much by pandering to this frenzy.

1374. So, to those who indulge in rage, let us be clear and speak directly.

1375. The furies possess you!

1376. You bring rampage to the weak and undeserving.

1377. You are aroused to your anger, even quietly waiting for the slightest provocation.

1378. You cite your entitlement, vengeance, and revenge as cause.

1379. You blame others and your pain.

1380. You have not learnt to let go, to set free, or to sacrifice.

1381. You have not learnt humility.

1382. Sometimes you offer a short-lived apology.

1383. Sometimes you secretly wish you weren't this person.

1384. Yet, I have nothing but *Aroha* for you, as we all should for each other.

1385. It is love unbounded.

1386. But you cannot grasp it.

1387. So you unleash the beast.

1388. Yes, I know there is no shade.

1389. I know you are broken.

1390. I also know you did not break yourself.

1391. I stand away.

1392. Come, stand back here with me. Let us watch this beast together.

1393. Watch it now with distance as your companion. Do not avert your gaze.

1394. All I see is anger personified, flailing around like a buffoon.

1395. What do you see?

1396. It is time to know the wisdom of our Ancestors.

1397. Your uncontrolled anger damages the *Te Ira Tangata* and *Te Ira Atua*, the Infinite Thread and the Sacred Tapestry that connects us all, to us all.

1398. You were dragged off your sacred thread. Thrown unceremoniously to the side.

1399. We want you back. We want all of you. We want you to be the best you can be.

1400. And now I ask just one thing.

1401. Step back onto it.

Insight 73: Riria te Riri. When Rage is Warranted.

1402. The oceans and rivers call you to move quickly, for there is a skirmish afoot.

1403. *Nga Waka Taua*, the War Canoes, are prepared.

1404. When it is time to act with force, let it only be when rage is warranted and matched against a worthy foe.

1405. *He riri, he riri, he toa, he toa! Tapatapa ruru ana te kakau o te hoe!*

1406. From the battle a brave warrior comes forth!

1407. The adrenalin surges mightily through your veins.

1408. Tis courage manifesting in the shudder of your paddle's handle!

Insight 74: Tumanako. Love's Hope.

1409. She holds out for the One.

1410. You know which one.

1411. She set herself aside for him.

1412. Her *Whaia-i-po*, her soul mate, her lover, the one she dreams of pursuing when night's amorous veil tumbles gently upon her desires.

1413. Many suitors approach, but she turns them away, because she wants to ensure her availability.

1414. But he does not come.

1415. In time, she suspects she has waited too long.

1416. She realises she has discarded real love for a delusion.

1417. Misplaced. Wasted. Naive.

1418. Kia ata tuku mai, kai mohu ana to ringa toro mai, paheke rawa i taku tinana.

1419. Ka kai ra e aku kanohi te kurumatarerehu.

1420. Hei te tau awhi te kino i aku mata.

1421. The Ancients say she was set aside, that is, she was *Puhi*, the Untouched Aristocracy.

1422. The arrival of three suitors deter her not, even though she can barely conceal her admiring glances.

1423. She succumbs neither to their touch nor to the temptations of nobility etched on their faces—nor even by the unexpected love she has come to feel for one.

1424. No. She rejects them for the One she waits for.

1425. He does not come.

1426. He pari horo au. I puhia reretia te tihi tapu.

1427. She is the virgin peak atop the crumbling cliff.

1428. She is battered by storm's indifference.

1429. Time passes, and she still shuns the adoring hopefuls who hover in her vicinity.

1430. But now their numbers dwindle.

1431. Soon, the distance between her and any semblance of love will pass beyond the point of retrieval.

1432. And still, he does not come.

Insight 75: Turchu. Aroha Hauaitu. Faeries. Superficial Love.

1433. We want to believe him when he says appearances are not at the fore, when he chooses his significant life partner.

1434. Yet, he barely disguises his delight when he notices the adoring stares from others.

1435. Confirming he has the kind of rare male charm that attracts beauteous creatures such as this one on his arm.

1436. But what of her? Does she celebrate his shallow disposition?

1437. Be assured, she wonders about a future when one day her alluring features will abandon her, leaving only the prevailing beauty of her wisdom, her journey, and her heart.

1438. She ponders whether he will be drawn away because of his failure to see the beauty within.

1439. The faery people, the *Turehu*, are not of our world and not of our people.

1440. They are of the mystical night.

1441. Their hair is red and their skin pale.

1442. The *Turehu* daughter, *Parearohi,* was chosen to ensure good relations between humans and faeries.

1443. So, she took *Heiraura* as her husband.

1444. In his world, *Parearohi* was confined to the darkness of the night.

1445. In the early mornings she would return to her people.

1446. However, *Heiraura* was a man who craved to see the likeness of his wife.

1447. One night, he blocked the chinks of his house as she slept.

1448. Day came, and she awoke late and distressed.

1449. By the light, he saw how fine-looking she was.

1450. However, he did not see that her physical beauty was of no consequence to her.

1451. He did not see the hurt in her eyes from broken trust.

1452. He immediately set out to gather his friends, so he could indulge in their praise—for he had made a great conquest and they should all know.

1453. The dignity of a woman does not necessarily diminish when she has been wronged.

1454. *Parearohi* composed herself.

1455. She affixed her husband's red feather plume to her head and emerged from the house. She climbed to the roof in full view and sang.

1456. Oh, *Heiraura* strutted about as his friends' admirations slid over him like the oily perfume of the *Raukawa*.

1457. Once her song was done, *Parearohi* pointed out to sea calling, There, there, there it goes!

1458. Her audience turned to look, but when they turned back, the *Turehu* daughter was gone.

1459. *E moea iho nei, kia tia taku rangi te rau o te amokura, tikapa ote auora ko nuku te rangi.*

1460. You will see me only in your dreams. Let me adorn my head with the plume of the fine *Amokura* and compose my thoughts while the sun is at its meridian, because it, like me, will descend ... and I will be gone.

Insight 76: Karakia Aroha. Love Charm.

1461. This one is for the menfolk who favour the womenfolk.

1462. Or the womenfolk who favour the menfolk.

1463. Or any folk who favour any folk.

1464. Please feel at liberty to change the gender-language below.

1465. Kia u te manawa-rere.

1466. Be still your racing heart.

1467. I assume you have sufficiently examined your intentions and have assured yourself of your good character before going any further.

1468. I do not wish to be responsible for unleashing a man who is overwrought with love but no sense.

1469. The *Tuahine*, Sisters, they deserve only the best.

1470. Consider yourself cautioned.

1471. You have had your eye on the woman of your dreams, your soul mate, your desire, for some time now.

1472. You have swaggered in front of her, flashed your dashing smile, and attempted to engage her in riveting conversation.

1473. Sadly, she remains unaware of your attentions.

1474. Surely, another will win her favour before she has had the opportunity to properly appreciate your finer points.

1475. Well, my friend, the faint-hearted never won the fair maiden.

1476. You can either rise to the challenge or slink away like the outgoing tide.

1477. It so happens the *Tupuna*, Ancestors, knew exactly how to remedy this tricky situation.

1478. There were many *Atahu*, Love Charms, available to a man to cause a woman to fall in love with him—if his previous attempts had failed.

1479. Before we begin, you must complete an errand.

1480. You have three tasks to choose from but only need to complete one.

1481. The first, place a small bundle of aromatic plants into her mouth when she is sleeping, the second, make a circlet with said plants so she might sit upon it, or the third, secretly place a feather in her hair.

1482. Of course, you may need to research the properties of the plant before placing it in her mouth.

1483. You may also want to check the legal implications of being in her bed-chamber if she has not invited you.

1484. Also, be aware certain breeds of birds are considered endangered. To have in your possession a feather from, say, a rare native bird, could result in your arrest.

1485. Once you have completed your task, the *Atahu* should be recited.

1486. In the interests of your success, and with my best wishes, I break protocol and provide you with the full charm.

1487. *Tapui aha taku tapui nei? Tapui tarata.*

1488. *Tapui aha taku tapui nei? Tapui taketake.*

1489. *Tapui aha taku tapui nei? Tapui huruhuru manu.*

1490. *Pera hoki ra tapu Nuku, tapu Rangi.*

1491. *O ki, o ki te reo o ko tangi te wai korito!*

1492. O, what charm is this charm of mine? It is a charm of the perfumed plants and the feather of a bird. Its potency is likened to the sacred powers of Earth and Sky. This, my voice, activates it!

1493. Oh yes, the scented leaves of the fragrant plant or the beauteous feather of a sweet bird, or perchance the feather dipped into the scented oil for extra potency, will surely bring you the love you deserve.

1494. And if not, then you, my friend, will need to look elsewhere.

Insight 77: He Tangata Ware Noa. A Nobody.

1495. We notice that those who are closest to us, fail to accept us.

1496. We receive no encouragement, no words of support, and no affirmations.

1497. It is as if we are *Tangata ware noa*, a Nobody.

1498. We try harder to be noticed. We over-compensate.

1499. Our behaviour is less than authentic because we do things to impress others or to avoid jealousy.

1500. In one moment, we hide our achievements for fear of criticism, and in the next, we display them in the hope of acceptance.

1501. We want to be important, or at least, important enough.

1502. We are confused and miserable.

1503. We struggle against the universe.

1504. We have not realised we have made it impossible for ourselves.

1505. *Kia eke koe ki runga kite puna o Tinirau!*

1506. We may as well be sitting upon the blowhole of the whale!

1507. We have created weakness because we grip so steadfastly to our desire for praise and endorsement.

1508. Now, it has become easy to nudge us off the slippery back of the whale.

1509. What lies at the heart of it?

1510. Our need to be loved? you offer.

1511. I say it is our sense of self-importance and it is leading us down a wretched path!

1512. It is time to let go.

1513. Know our purpose, the reason we are here—the thing that ignites our heart.

1514. Know it. Live it. Make every task relevant to it.

1515. When we take on a new task, ask whether we are doing it because we want approval.

1516. Discard the tasks motivated by people-pleasing.

1517. We do not need their admiration, acceptance or validation.

1518. Our path must be free from the desire for glory, acknowledgement, and confirmation.

1519. Let our actions be unnoticed.

1520. Let us set ourselves free from this unnecessary pain, so we can get on with meeting our full capability.

1521. Let us serve our purpose meticulously.

1522. *Ae, kia eke koe ki runga kite puna o Tinirau!*

1523. It is enough that we ride upon the back of a magnificent whale on the great ocean of *Tangaroa*.

1524. Who cares whether there is anyone on the shore to see?

Insight 78: Mauri Rere. Whakaiti. Panic. Vulnerability.

1525. The old manuscripts tell of the arrival of *Tohoraha*, the Southern Right Whale, who brings with her the *Mana*, prestige, power, and potency, of the old esoteric knowledge.

1526. You paddle a *Waka*, Canoe, upon the sea.

1527. The coast is to your left and the open ocean to your right.

1528. You go with conviction towards some worthy cause.

1529. Suddenly, you realise your paddle is no longer touching the ocean's surface.

1530. You lean to look over the side.

1531. To your horror, *Tohoraha* has swum underneath and lifted your *Waka* above the surface of the water.

1532. You only paddle salty air!

1533. It is a sign. Look directly into her eye.

1534. She is here to remind you.

1535. Your vulnerability is easily exposed when a greater force threatens.

1536. The trail is crossed with many challenges.

1537. Do not panic, do not let go of your paddle, you will need it.

1538. *E hoa, tera ara te ara whakawhiti i nga wero maha. Ka eke koe ma runga waka, me mau kaha i to hoe. Kia kaua koe e wareware te panekeneke me te panukunuku, ka hoe kaha koe hei toa, hei tae atu ki to whainga.*

Insight 79: Whakaarorangi. Intention.

1539. The old manuscripts give an ancient *Karakia*, Invocation, uttered by the Great Navigator *Kupe*.

1540. Along with the strongest and ablest of his Kin, he prepared to embark on an epic voyage from his island homeland of *Hawaiki-Rangi* to new lands across the formidable southern ocean, *Te Moana-Nui-A-Kiwa*, the Pacific Ocean.

1541. No frail elders, no children, no weak members— only the fittest and those who could continue the progeny.

1542. And only the *Tohunga*, Knowledge-Keepers, whose expertise was of direct benefit.

1543. We often forget when we retell these tales of courage and adversity that the heroes were just people.

1544. So, let us not pretend the Great Navigator is some kind of demi-god, perfect in character and infallible.

1545. Let us tell it as it was.

1546. The dire circumstances that compelled *Kupe* and his people to leave on such a perilous journey were of his making.

1547. He was an adventurer and a strategist, but it was his treachery that led them all to this day.

1548. The significant ocean crossing to a land that only existed in legends seemed insurmountable.

1549. Once they were out at sea, there would be a critical point of no return.

1550. Is it no wonder then, back there on the beach, trepidation found its roots in the hearts of his Kinfolk?

1551. The Navigator was acutely aware of the enormity of the task and the smallness of his capability.

1552. So, he unleashed his full intention to where *Atua*, the Great Immortals, and their powers awaited.

1553. They would not waste their response on frivolous purposes.

1554. If actualised, it would be an extraordinary collaboration not rivalled since the separation of the original parents, Sky and Earth!

1555. The *Atua*, Great Immortals, would not simply gather to save *Kupe* from his demise. Neither to provide the *Mokopuna*, Grandchildren, with a hero.

1556. But, it was time for the people to find the spiritual homeland of their future.

1557. Before the explorers from the North came and heaved their worldviews onto the beaches.

1558. So, the *Atua* congregated.

1559. *Kupe* was their pawn.

1560. He inherently knew this, but still had to convince them of his conviction.

1561. So, he stood and directed the Great Immortals as if his command were rule.

1562. *E tu mai nei! Hikihiki Rangi kite tauihu rape nui o Tane!*

1563. His voice boomed.

1564. Stand! Rise up, Sky, and make way for this mystical canoe!

1565. Oh, dear reader, your heart must be in your throat!

1566. You cannot wait to hear what happens next.

Insight 80: Whakarangatira. Ennoble.

1567. When her loved one is taken, she has no wish to compare.

1568. Yet, she thinks of the rare and lustrous plume of the exquisite *Huia*, the Heteralocha Acutirostris.

1569. That feather will no longer adorn her head.

1570. She thinks of the noble flight of *Toroa*, the Albatross, who will go to the northern-most tip of this land, to *Te Rerenga Wairua*.

1571. It is where the two oceans meet and where those who have passed go to take their final leap into the next realm.

1572. Here, her beloved will enter the numinous waters and navigate his passage back to the ancient homelands.
1573. She laments.
1574. Ehara ite taane, he huia tu ra, he toroa whakakopa ra runga onga hiwi. Taku manu korero, tiu ana ki te muri e.
1575. You were more than a husband. You were my foremost *huia*-plume, an albatross in flight o'er the high ridges. Alas, my renowned bird flies to the farthest north.

SECTION 9: WOMEN AND MEN

Insight 81: Taurite Tuatahi. Wahine. Tane. Balance First. Female. Male.

1576. I learnt that balance is the optimal state.

1577. I had to let go of some chunky grudges. My victimhood. My anger.

1578. I had to 'see' my brothers. And my sisters.

1579. It is too easy to take a side, to belittle one while uplifting the other.

1580. The *Tohunga,* Sage, says there is a female essence for every male essence.

1581. It starts with *Papatuanuku*, Earth Mother, and *Ranginui*, Sky Father.

1582. Then to humans.

1583. In this context, the sexes only become relevant when the potential of one is obstructed.

1584. So, the insights address obstructed potential, and sometimes speak to the men, sometimes the women.

1585. If they do not exude empathy, I have failed in my duty.

Insight 82:Tohunga-Wahine. Tohunga-Tane. Female and Male Sages.

1586. The *Tohunga*, Sage, wrote.

1587. Ko nga korero mo te Tohungatanga.

1588. E rua nga turanga Tohunga.

1589. Ko te turanga tohunga Taane ka tahi.

1590. Ko te turanga tohunga Wahine ka rua.

1591. There are two mainstays of esoteric knowledge.

1592. One is the bastion of men.

1593. The other is the bastion of women.

1594. There is no hierarchy.

1595. No need to compare.

1596. No need to stake out the best position.

Insight 83: Te Kaha o te Wahine. Power in Women.

1597. Let me beckon the men over.

1598. The ancient knowledge in the manuscripts is a stark contrast to that in some academic books.

1599. In an aggressive display of patriarchal privilege, the early European scholars and missionaries annulled *Maori* women as Knowledge-Keepers.

1600. They were omitted from all accounts of spiritual, intellectual, and political matters.

1601. Our women were recast as *naïve simpletons, virgin maidens, witches, shamans,* and *cacodemons.*

1602. You think I am using exaggerated language?

1603. My brother, those are not my words.

1604. They can be found in well-worn publications sitting on the shelves of arrogant scholarship.

1605. The ancient knowledge written by our old people is free from such meddling.

1606. They reveal women are Knowledge-Keepers of the highest calibre.

1607. They are not constrained when the call for action comes.

1608. The Illustrious *Kuia*, Ancient Grandmothers, fought, rescued, sacrificed, outsmarted, and performed their callings under the mantles of *Tumatauenga*, War, and *Rongo*, Peace.

1609. Do not believe for a moment that a woman's reticence is some desired inherent attribute or appropriate behaviour.

1610. So now I clarify.

1611. This is not about women in power, but the power in women.

1612. This is not about politics and the feminist movement, but *Mana Wahine*, women's intrinsic prestige, power, and potency.

1613. If we continue to adopt thinly disguised *tikanga*, processes and protocols, that curtail the full potential and participation of women, then we inadvertently, or perhaps deliberately, become an ally of the Colonisers.

1614. This is not about you. Or me. It is about us. All of us.

1615. Challenge your brothers and fathers.

1616. Share your seats of entitlement.

1617. Bring the women from the floor to the armchairs.

1618. Be attentive when they speak in the realm of *Tumatauenga*, the Realm of Fighting Talk. They don't do it lightly.

1619. Do so without offence, anger, ignorance or fear.

1620. Instigate change. Step up. Make room. Recalibrate.

1621. I am done.

Insight 84: Tai-Tama-Wahine. Tai-Tama-Taane. Female and Male Tides.

1622. Sisters, look to the edge of the tide, to the enduring ebb and flow of *Tai-Tama-Wahine*, the Feminine East Tides, and *Tai-Tama-Taane*, the Masculine West Tides.

1623. There are still those of us who believe respect for our menfolk requires our silence. Our passivity. Our pleasing.

1624. We give him the voice and the decisions. We prop him up. We repair the damage. We apologise for him. We defend him. We flatter him.

1625. In all these acts, we are misled.

1626. He does not need any of this from us.

1627. When *Tai-Tama-Wahine* does not fully join the tidal cycle, *Tai-Tama-Taane* rolls in unfettered, wild, and deluded.

1628. We wait, believing the thrashing waters will eventually produce some benefit for all.

1629. We will be waiting forever.

1630. *Tane ma*, men, you have encroached upon the beach.

1631. Prepare to roll your Tides back, and join the cycle.

1632. *Wahine ma*, women, it is time to bring forth your Tides to the shore.

Insight 85: Te Whatitiri. Celestial Grandmother of Thunder.

1633. In many *Karakia*, Invocations, *Te Whatitiri*, the Celestial Grandmother of Thunder, is the first to be summoned.

1634. *Papa Te Whatitiri!*

1635. Her resounding boom is not just for dramatic effect.

1636. Her voice alerts us to an imminent revelation.

1637. But she has been reduced to a by-line, no explanation, no insight.

1638. The story of the journey to receive knowledge for humankind popularised by religious and colonial scholars, tells of the dashing *Tane-nui-a-rangi*, the supreme god *Io*, the heavens, and the victory of good over evil.

1639. In this Christian-like account, there is no prominent place for a *blind old crone* like *Te Whatitiri*.

1640. Her celestial boom is not heard from amidst the rabble of lesser beings.

1641. She has been silenced.

1642. In a less publicised version of the account, the blind and powerful *Te Whatitiri* is the Sage-Grandmother of *Tawhaki.*

1643. It is She, not *Io,* who guards the knowledge.

1644. She does not occupy one of the ten or twelve or twenty heavens—there is no need for such hierarchy and elitism in this account.

1645. Her lack of sight is no hindrance.

1646. It is not necessary to see knowledge with the eyes.

1647. *Te Whatitiri* gives *Tawhaki* the knowledge for humankind because she knows he is in unison with the genetic thread that connects him to her, and which also connects us to the other Great Immortals, to each other, and to the animals, stars, rocks, rivers, and mountains.

1648. The Tapestry.

1649. *Tawhaki* stands firmly upon a Thread.

1650. A belief that claims there is a need for an aloof and supreme god is one that often suppresses the full potential and power of the Feminine.

1651. And silences our celestial Grandmothers.

SECTION 10: THE WORLD

Insight 86: Nga Ao e Maramatia ana. Worldviews.

1652. There is remarkable knowledge passed on by generations of my people, but it has been largely locked away.

1653. Today is the day to bring it out into the light.

1654. Some have asked, is our knowledge more or less than those of other peoples?

1655. Let us refrain from comparing.

1656. There is no need to support the idea that one culture's knowledge is superior or not. It leads us down a terrible path.

1657. The knowledge is part of the spectrum that adds to our collective contributions.

1658. What an incredible world we have together.

Insight 87: Pakanga. Battle.

1659. The *Taua*, War Party, come. Hundreds.

1660. Tall, athletic, heavy-built men.

1661. But they do not move as the Northern Hemispherites do, in beat, ordered marching, exact stance, posture, all in the manner of each of the men around them, straight lines, perfect replication, arms swinging exactly so-and-so and a half-inch's distance from the middle of the thigh, to the rear, then to the fore, matching plastic-moulded soldiers.

1662. It can be observed at any distance.

1663. The *Taua* move in unison across the land too, keeping formation, but without the tell-tale beat.

1664. This mass of fighting men advances with the creeping motion of a large reptile.

1665. Nice.

1666. But I do not care for war.

1667. Worshippers of force.

1668. There has been too much hacking and hewing across every continent for millennia.

1669. It is surely the most corrupt and inane manner of acquiring wealth—thinly disguised as honour.

Insight 88: Hanga Marore. Delicate Dispositions.

1670. Before going any further, I implore the reader who does not understand our people's morality—especially in the old times—to resist forming a poor opinion.

1671. You may have a delicateness about you. A squeamish constitution.

1672. The consequence of too much refinement.

1673. This may cause you to come to the most erroneous of conclusions.

1674. I hope now you have taken a moment, that I have adequately prepared you for the next *Insight*.

Insight 89: Tangata Ngaro. Stragglers and Runaways.

1675. It is said this land was the last to be drawn on the world map.

1676. Well, aside from Antarctica.

1677. By the early-1800s, a few European ships had made it past *Nga Taniwha*, the Dragons, and swerved off just in time to avoid *Te Mata o te Ao*, the Edge of the World.

1678. I tease.

1679. Ships came and went, some only passed by, some landed, and some ran away, I mean, sailed away. At speed.

1680. There was bloodshed.

1681. The newcomers included runaways from the whaling ships—whose method of arrival by sneaking in was considered particularly ill-mannered by our people.

1682. But then again, likely they were escaping a ruthless regime.

1683. These men lived in a vile state.

1684. Their own countrymen considered them to be far greater savages than the natives.

1685. To our people, a straggler or runaway without endearing qualities was of no account.

1686. Perhaps he could aptly lend his hand to local battles.

1687. But if he had no kin, no prospects, no leg to stand on, no anything, then what was his use?

1688. Would he just eat his way through unearned food?

1689. Suffice to say, he would not last long in this place.

1690. Pot to fire. Fire to pot.

1691. But that is another story for a much hardier reader.

Insight 90: Kore Kai Tangata. How Not To Get Eaten.

1692. My four Greats followed by Grandfather was an Irishman.

1693. He arrived in these islands in 1833 from Dublin via Tasmania, Van Diemen's Land as it was known then.

1694. Like all new immigrants, he was initially oblivious to his general worth.

1695. Clearly, he was not one of those aforementioned runaways, but a man of some means, evidenced by his frockcoat, top hat, and double-barrelled gun.

1696. As his little schooner left the ship for shore, he asked himself whether the crowd of natives in the distance might be less than friendly—he'd heard stories.

1697. However, his face and demeanour showed no anxiety, for fear can be concealed with the right amount of determined grit.

1698. But there, he was nearing the shore and could see at least three of his Kinsmen standing amongst them.

1699. Alive and smiling.

1700. Surely a good sign.

1701. In any case, the underside of his boat scraped against the sand, and it was too late to do anything but put on as unconcerned a countenance as possible.

1702. These were early days in occupation.

1703. Lawfulness for immigrants had not yet been established, and there was a roughness about the place.

1704. The value of an immigrant to a tribe could be enormous, or not.

1705. There were stragglers and runaways everywhere! No value at all.

1706. But a good Trader was worth twenty times his weight in muskets.

1707. A newly acquired Trader was to be treasured and safeguarded—and given a high-value wife carefully selected for strategic tribal and commercial advantages.

1708. If not properly cared for, a newly acquired Trader could be killed, have an accident, run away, or be robbed.

1709. This would not be advantageous at all.

1710. He might take his goods away.

1711. His relations could come to seek revenge.

1712. Oh, you must know by now my four Greats followed by Grandfather was worth his weight in muskets and more, or your author wouldn't be here to write this book.

Insight 91: Nga Mea Maumaharatanga. Monuments.

1713. We wonder why our *Tupuna*, Ancestors, refrained from building large spiritual monuments.

1714. They did not build pillars, pulpits, statues or golden shrines.

1715. At most, they assembled modest focal points, but more often there was no trace.

1716. Why do we feel compelled to build grand monuments in the name of our beliefs—upsized indulgence on the landscape?

1717. Surely, there is no human-made monument that can surpass those already adorning the body of *Papa-tua-nuku*, Earth Mother.

1718. Are not the mountains, oceans, and rivers monument enough?

1719. The outward expression of the old people's spirituality was not represented by grand things.

1720. Those surely are evidence of faiths that have become outwardly concerned with appearances.

1721. Symbols of materialism, obsession, importance, control, oppression, and contradiction.

1722. And below their beautifully crafted walls, the suffering lie in the gutters.

Insight 92: Tangata Kohuku. Purakau. One-Dimensional Characters. Myths.

1723. Our myths have been invaded.

1724. The stories skewed.

1725. The complex personalities suppressed.

1726. One-dimensional characters devoid of nuances.

1727. When the stories are fully told, we realise there is neither evil nor good, no angels or devils, just shades and shadows, and hues and textures.

1728. The characters are busy making chaos, exercising their muscles, maybe teaching us a lesson worth learning. Then they're gone. A gust across our face.

1729. The old manuscripts tell of multidimensional characters, some with inconsistent and questionable motives.

1730. They all have one thing in common.

1731. To incrementally increase the proportion of happiness in their lives.

1732. Even the nastiest ones.

1733. They strive to do what they believe is right or best.

1734. Yet, we are denied the full backstory.

1735. When we are told the *Toa*—Hero, seeks good for all.

1736. Observe.

1737. We notice he is impulsive, and his ego drives him.

1738. Yet, the positive results of his actions, whether by design or not, bring him fame, and we gladly bestow glory upon him.

1739. He is chuffed. His grin stretches from one end of the horizon to the other.

1740. We are told the *Kuia*—Illustrious Grandmother, is an ugly sorceress who is determined to do evil upon an unsuspecting hero.

1741. The recurring story of the malevolent woman and unsuspecting man reinforces our indoctrination.

1742. So, we do not discover the Crone's mission is to protect knowledge that may alter the course of history.

1743. She will not relinquish it to one who is greedy or unprepared for its power.

1744. If provoked, she will inflict a severe punishment. So be it.

1745. We are told of the *one son* who separated his parents to bring *Te Ao Marama,* Enlightenment, into our world. His strong back. His strong legs. His utter power.

1746. The other son, the one with the unrelenting loyalty, is given a cameo role.

1747. Yet, his love was so absolute, he was willing to live in Darkness so his parents could be together in love forever. An example for us all.

1748. And now? He wreaks havoc on all of us for his brother's betrayal.

1749. It was never going to be that black and white.

1750. We are told this *sweet young thing* is *Puhi*—the Maiden.

1751. This is the Coloniser's word for 'virgin', a coveted prize for an uncouth man with extra coins in his pocket.

1752. Our heroine has been cast so because her untouched purity and, of course, the attraction of a potential conquest, coupled with her feeble-mind, fulfils a particular agenda.

1753. Let us truly see her.

1754. In the moment she perceives a threat, she swiftly transforms from gentle nurturer and protector, to warrior.

1755. After the commotion, she does not wait for praise but stoops to gather the scattered pieces and restore calm.

1756. Enough. We can work the rest out for ourselves.

Insight 93: Hereheretia, Wetewete. Binding, Loosening.

1757. Inadequacy, competitiveness, uncertainty and fear—all characteristics of the ego-mind that is overly concerned with itself.

1758. When we hope to look good or save face, we elevate our ego to first position and lower our task to second.

1759. The *Tupuna*, Ancestors, sought to treat certain tasks with great observance and consideration.

1760. When commitment was required, inadequacy, competitiveness, uncertainty, and fear were not granted a position.

1761. Conviction was.

1762. The Binding is a collaborative effort between *Atua*, the Great Immortals, and people, to ensure the task's success.

1763. The task is made *Tapu*—under the influence of *Atua*.

1764. We loosen the task from what is destructive.

1765. And bind it to what is life-giving.

1766. Only the necessary elements are bound together. No more. No less.

1767. Not glory, not accolades, not awards.

1768. But optimal conditions—calm seas, clear skies, right people, right time.

1769. Various *Karakia*, Invocations, in the old manuscripts illustrate the method of binding particular *Atua* to particular tasks.

1770. The Binding first affirms the protection and power of an *Atua*.

1771. Then the necessary conditions for success.

1772. It ensures all participants bring their full capacity to the task.

1773. Renowned Navigator *Kupe* bound no less than seven *Atua* to the journey across the Great Ocean of *Kiwa*, *Te Moana-Nui-a-Kiwa*, the Pacific Ocean.

1774. Their combined capacity matched the magnitude of the task and what he believed was necessary to achieve it.

1775. For less daunting tasks, you may only need to bind one *Atua*.

1776. They are identified and commanded—never petitioned.

1777. *Tena te hau, ko te hau o Rongo.*

1778. *E Rongo, mau ki tenei mahi.*

1779. Behold, the vital essence of *Rongo-ma-tane*, the Great Immortal of Peaceful Endeavours.

1780. *Rongo*, hold fast to this task.

1781. Once the task is complete, a loosening occurs, through a final *Karakia*, Invocation.

1782. It is confirmed that the task has been fulfilled.

1783. *Takiritia ra, whakanoatia, whakahekea, ko maiea nga atua, maiea nga tangata, ko maiea.*

1784. Let it loose, free it from restrictions, let it down.

1785. All is satisfied and acknowledged.

1786. Then, food is consumed to return us to our daily lives.

1787. And now the task is released from the influence of *Atua*.

1788. It is no longer *Tapu*.

1789. It is done.

Insight 94: Taniwha. Supernatural Creatures.

1790. Some say, the *Taniwha*, Supernatural Creatures with a Mission, is a faery-tale and the imaginings of an inferior savage culture.

1791. *Taniwha* are of the land, the sky, and the sea.

1792. They are international travellers, tending to ocean-going voyages.

1793. Some possess great *Mana*, prestige, power, and potency.

1794. Some are hostile, others helpful.

1795. They may take the form of floating logs, reptiles, whales—or beasts that inhabit your nightmares.

1796. *Taniwha* do not purely exist to inflict fear.

1797. They guard lakes, waterfalls, springs, and caves.

1798. They protect locations, ecosystems, and treasures.

1799. They are obsessed. It is their strength.

1800. They never deviate from their task.

1801. They do not wander from the vicinity of their charge.

1802. They are vigilant.

1803. They sleep with one eye on you.

1804. It is said, if we pose no risk, the *Taniwha* will leave us be.

1805. But should we pose a danger, they will react quickly, springing from the shadows to eliminate the threat.

1806. The *Taniwha* represents the guardianship that has been abandoned long ago by those who prefer to spill their waste into waterways and ravage the land in favour of progress and development.

1807. Many will think it silly.

1808. No-one has seen a *Taniwha* and produced the evidence.

1809. We could rightly assume that they are all dead or, at least, lying low.

1810. Perchance they wait for some powerful *Tohunga*, Sage, to call them to action.

1811. I tell you, it has been a very long time since one of that calibre has spoken.

1812. So, we may never see the scales on the back of a *Taniwha*, but we might stumble upon its lair.

1813. And to those of you who insist you glimpsed the swishing tail in the moment before it disappeared below the murky water, be satisfied that it did no more than show itself and did not consider you a threat.

Insight 95: 葉落歸根. Nga Rau Ngahoro. Falling Leaves.

1814. Back then, my people had only met the white colonial administrators, traders, and runaways.

1815. They had not yet met the non-European world.

1816. Those people had not yet poured into these northern parts.

1817. So, on a Spring morning in 1902, their surprise must have surely surpassed any other to date.

1818. There they stood, amidst coffins and shrouded bodies strewn along the beach, with the sea mist hiding those further away from view.

1819. My people knew not who they were, except they were not from this place.

1820. The etchings on some of the coffins were exquisite, surely indicating some were *Rangatira*, Noble Ones.

1821. It was posited by the Elders that they be interred in the *Waahi Tapu*, Burial Grounds, atop the sacred hill.

1822. Despite the Missionaries' influence on their Leader who decreed only converts were allowed there now.

1823. Not this time.

1824. This time the mysterious arrivals would be buried with our people.

1825. For they were *Tupapaku*, devoid of life, and *Manuhiri*, visitors, of the most unusual kind.

1826. They would be cared for until their people came. One day.

1827. So, they were interred alongside our *Tupuna*, Ancestors, on the hill.

1828. On Mount Zion.

1829. The story was passed down and down.

1830. Too short a time to become mythology, and too long a time to sound entirely believable.

1831. They will come, said the old people.

1832. A hundred years passed. And more.

1833. Then they came.

1834. The Chinese descendants told their story.

1835. The unusual cargo of 499 deceased Chinese was being returned from the deep South of our islands, where gold glinted in the eyes of the entrepreneurs and where Chinese men had been shipped in by the thousands—to dig.

1836. The work was hard. They worked for years. Many died on our soil.

1837. Their bodies were stored until a steamship could return them to their families in the province of Poon Yue, Guangdong (romanticised as Canton), China.

1838. Tragically, they were shipwrecked ten miles off our northern coast, *Hokianga*.

1839. Where my people watched them float ashore.

1840. The Chinese have a saying.

1841. 葉落歸根

1842. Falling leaves settle on their roots. Everything reverts to its original source.

1843. The grief their people, carried for generations, was eventually brought to our burial grounds, lifetimes later.

1844. Some solace was found, but it would never be fully resolved.

1845. The leaves had not returned to their roots.

1846. Back on the beach that day in 1902, my *Tupuna*, Ancestors, saw that now the white man had acquired sovereignty over their lands, the rest of the world would come.

1847. And they could not prevent the dual tides of opportunity and exploitation from rolling in with every ship.

1848. Even so, their choice in these circumstances was to show *Manaakitanga*, kindness, generosity, and caring of others.

1849. That was the year *The Old Man* began writing.

SECTION 11: WHAT NEXT?

Insight 96: He Kaupapa Nunui. Something Bigger.

1850. The *Tohunga*, Sage, had a higher purpose, higher than himself.

1851. He spent his life capturing the essence of it.

1852. Honing it.

1853. It was powerful and authoritative.

1854. It was magic.

1855. That's why others coveted it.

1856. And now you think you might need it because, frankly, the world is a mess.

1857. *Grandchild, you cannot present your outstretched hand and expect to receive without effort.*

1858. *You have no entitlement.*

1859. *It requires your attention and courage.*

1860. *And you must overcome your adversaries.*

1861. *Starting with yourself.*

1862. It seems insurmountable, doesn't it?

1863. The gap between what he left behind and our ability to comprehend it today, is sizeable.

1864. It was not what he planned.

1865. But generations later, we are all he has.

1866. We are all we have.

Insight 97: Whakaora Ano te Tapu. Restore the Tapu.

1867. The old people say the *Tapu* is gone.

1868. We have lost our integrity.

1869. The insights demand we restore it.

1870. It is time to confront our beliefs.

1871. To address the condition of our *Mana*.

1872. To seek wisdom in the face of seemingly impossible odds.

1873. It is time to restore the *Tapu*.

Insight 98: Nga Mea Iti Nei. Small Things.

1874. Some believe we are witnessing the final throes of an inept phase in humanity.

1875. This, they say, has been brought about by insatiable greed, blind ignorance, and the insistent march of misguided enterprise and progress.

1876. It is signalled by the polluted rivers, the murky air, the depleted species, the horrific sufferings of people, and the widespread corrosion of human behaviour.

1877. Some ready themselves for the next evolutionary stage of human existence.

1878. The Old Man wrote.

1879. Te kaha te pekapeka a Nuku.

1880. Te kaha te pekapeka a Rangi.

1881. He says the shared *Mana*, prestige, power, and potency, of Earth and Sky Immortals, *Papa-tua-nuku* and *Rangi-nui*, is weakened.

1882. Those brandishing the most advanced new environmental sciences and technologies cannot solve issues of greed and irresponsibility.

1883. They merely mitigate the impacts—and only if forced.

1884. They fail to acknowledge their own recklessness.

1885. We resist delving too deeply into this irony because we may have to give up something we like—our luxuries.

1886. It is easier, is it not, to focus upon the lighter aspects of our lives?

1887. Do we not hold to the excuse that solutions to big problems are well beyond our means?

1888. There is nothing we can do to unravel the entangled mess.

1889. We hope for a miracle of mass decency.

1890. Surely a good old-fashioned crisis of magnitude is enough to change the world for good.

1891. Weather, war, virus, falling space debris?

1892. We've had a few already. I'm not sure they had the effect we hoped for.

1893. So, we are frozen.

1894. Still, the ache in our heart persists.

1895. What will we leave our Grandchildren?

1896. Haere mai, haere ki to matua ra nge, kia hikitia koe.

1897. The answers lie with those *Tupuna*, Ancestors of Merit, who long ago walked this earth leaving only light footprints.

1898. From them, we discover the only force of progress worth holding on to is *Aroha*, love unbounded and unending.

1899. *Aroha* alone leads to everything else we need. Every decision. Every result.

1900. It is the intrinsic understanding that the only force with *Mana* is that which embraces empathy, compassion, and kinship.

1901. Aiming for something as sentimental as *Aroha* is not easy.

1902. In today's cynical world we would certainly be labelled a goody two shoes, and then suddenly we're right back in the playground trying to prove we're cooler than that.

1903. It is not a question of our coolness, but of our confidence.

1904. *Aroha* is easy. It starts with small things. A way of responding once or twice, here and there. Soon consistently. Accumulating. Piling up. Gathering mass. Touching those within our reach.

1905. *Aroha* can be given without depleting the stockpile.

1906. It can be given without accolades, reward or payback.

1907. As my Grandmother used to say, *'If you do everything with Aroha in your heart, you will live a good life, and you will give others a good life.'*

1908. Let us not debilitate ourselves because we feel overwhelmed by the urgency of today's problems.

1909. Let us not shy away from taking responsibility for the solution.

1910. It is ours.

1911. The Ancestors remind us.

1912. I herea tutia te kaha o Rongomai.

1913. He iti mahinga na Rongomai e toto te oneone.

1914. *Rongomai* was steadfast.

1915. Even his seemingly small deeds had the Earth's life force running.

1916. What seems small can become sustaining.

1917. If we cannot do big things, then let us do many small things.

1918. Let us choose every small part of our life with the foresight of the Ancestors and *Aroha* for our Grandchildren.

Insight 99: Whakawatea. Cleaning Up.

1919. Now we have read, pondered, flipped pages back and forth, lost our place, read lines twice, thrice, skipped a few, guffawed, sobbed.

1920. Still deciding whether or not the insights moved us.

1921. Whether or not to clap.

1922. Irrespective, perhaps now is a good time to clean up our mess.

1923. Oh, we don't like to talk about our missteps.

1924. The mud we scrubbed off our knees.

1925. That's fine. We're looking ahead now.

1926. If we choose to clean up one small flaw at a time, we may come to tangibly know we are a slightly improved version of ourselves today, than we were yesterday.

1927. If we do, we'll change our future—all of our futures.

1928. Be warned. Some of those around us may not like it.

1929. We will step quietly past them.

1930. They will beg us to return.

1931. Then demand we don't betray them, the tribe.

1932. We will pull away. They will escalate.

1933. Eventually, it will be done, and we will have learnt something valuable.

1934. That a good life is founded on understanding our *Whanaungatanga*—Kinship, to everyone and everything.

1935. That our sense of purpose and values can drive our contribution to the world.

1936. That our contributions don't have to be the same.

1937. That if we want better results, we need to tell better stories—or tell the stories better.

1938. That we can seed a shared garden in the short time we are on this earth because there is no rational reason why every flower, tree, and weed cannot flourish if we choose to water it.

1939. That we are all here in this place together.

1940. And no-one is going anywhere.

Chapter Thirteen
What It Takes

A T THE BEGINNING I DID NOTHING. The Old Man was a revered *Tohunga*, Sage, of some standing in his time, and his memory had been further augmented with a series of surreal tales and a degree of idolism. His manuscripts had become renowned, and their disappearance for three generations was a mystery to most. I spent several years holding his manuscripts in care and challenging my right and ability to serve the intent of The Old Man and his peers. I had been taught (and told with no uncertainty) that *Putea Whakairo*, the old manuscripts with the deeper knowledge, were only for the chosen. I began looking for who the chosen one might be. I found two kinds of responses to my inquiries.

The first group were those who I approached amongst my relatives, elders, and others who I believed might contribute. They each had a similar response, saying they'd not been given the knowledge, they were born too late, some were afraid to breach *Tapu,* but they would support in any way they could. And they did this by way of sharing what they did know, personal encouragement, questioning, challenging, and being trusted confidants. Some of those beautiful souls are no longer with us.

I remain forever grateful to this group—*anei ra, e rere ake nei te aroha ki a koutou nga pou, Te Wananga Kakariki.*

The second group sought me out. These men used a variety of techniques in their attempts to win my favour. They flattered, promised, flirted, shared far too much of their so-called secret materials in the hope I'd share back, and talked themselves up a hundred miles an hour—all for a sneak peek at the manuscripts. I came to learn how to identify those whose goal was to elevate their 'mana' or to fortify their academic, religious or guruhood aspirations. None spoke of how the manuscripts, or their access to them, might serve our people. Not one.

Through these years of looking for someone, my inaction hid the truth. That I was afraid. I would suffer the consequences of breaching *Tapu*. I would be accused of acting above my station, both as a woman, and one from the junior line. I would be exposed as the wrong person, judged, and shunned.

In the meantime, my extended family were drifting further apart. Our home base, our land was gone, and our kinship was becoming tenuous. Religion, social and economic status, cultural connection, geographic distance, and lost identity were creating divides. Now, many of the next generation barely know who their relations are, barely know who they are, and have never heard of The Old Man and his legacy. Eventually, I realised if I did nothing, the next generation would find it impossible. The Grandchildren became my focus. And the task? To unshackle the fear, reveal the beauty of our legacy and our identity, and help us all rediscover our *Whanaungatanga*—Kinship.

So, to work. There was one book my relations had been told to strictly avoid by a man of influence in the wider tribe. He encouraged a kind of cowering fear and claimed he alone had the 'mana' to acquire and distribute the old knowledge. He told several that if they looked at any of the manuscripts, and especially a particular book, there would be terrible consequences. Some of my relations had already pulled me aside to warn me off, afraid for my 'spiritual safety', but also to tell me they were afraid of this man and his influence. Red flag. Bull.

Leadership is an interesting phenomenon. Even when a leader does not serve us, we follow if we perceive he or she has power— because being on the side of a bully is better than being hurt by one. We think we are under their protective arm, until one day we aren't. How foolish we can be.

Book two—the 'forbidden' text—would take me directly to face a fear that had been carefully stoked by others all my life. I turned the pages slowly as if each one might invoke a sudden strike of lightning. I kept turning until I came across a page that drew my attention. In one short extract, the words exposed the lies and the false fears my relations and I had been fed. It was a door to freedom. That page transformed everything.

You may ask which of the insights I am referring to. I found mine. You find your own.

I hadn't known yet that The Old Man had marked a trail within the thousands of pages, and all I had to do was follow. But as I turned the pages, I began to understand. So, I let him lead me into his world. When I eventually started writing, a torrent swept through me. I created pages and pages of words, drawings, shapes, and scribbles. Three months of intensive, obsessive production. A mosaic. Then, I converted that work into extracts, some of which appear in this book. I wrote faster than I could absorb them. It was a pivotal point. What I found changed me.

I had no reason to continue to cling to my limitations, insecurities, and inaction. I needed to step up—and further, I needed to honour the legacies left by my ancestors—swathed equally in their suffering and their foresight. I began to assimilate the insights that most resonated—one by one. Each was a discrete destination of its own. I'm still working through them.

We tend to put sages in a kind of mystical, super-human category. But my Elders who shared their stories told how they interacted with The Old Man in real ways, ranging from indifference to reverence. He was not just some inaccessible, awe-inspiring sage; he was also my great-grandfather, a man with talents and flaws who lived on a farm with cows and chickens, and who wrote obsessively with a lead pencil. Thinking of him in this way makes it easier to imagine our conversations—to chuckle at his understated humour, see the sharp wit in his eyes, and sense his low tolerance for my dithering (I swiftly relegate dithering to my back pocket). When tackling a difficult question, I just ask what The Old Man would say.

Comfortable in his armchair he holds the hot cup in both hands. Steam rises. Speckled sun plays on tiny droplets. Worn jacket wraps loosely around his wiry frame. Looks vaguely out the window. Waits.

I ponder.

I ask whether any of this will matter in a hundred years.

I think it will. Time will tell.

Are the insights merely artefacts from the past or guidelines for our future?

What do I do with them? I don't say it out loud, but he hears it.

He turns. Eyes. Deep pools.

Tohaina atu ra enei kupu e Ko.

Share the words.

I'm silent. It's too big.

I don't know if I can. It's barely a whisper.

He leans in. Rough hand on mine, still warm from the cup.

Ka taea ngawaritia noatia.

You have what it takes.

His *Aroha* drifts between us. In this moment my fears dissolve.

Ah yes, of course, this is about choice—not capability.

The part of me that cannot resist rising to a challenge looks up.

His expression changes. And now I am looking at a man who is looking at me with absolute confidence. As if he's seeing me for the first time. We are mirrors.

Tena ko koe.

There you are, he chuckles.

Insight 100: Te Wehenga. The Parting.

1941. We have arrived. We came this far together and did not part ways.

1942. Surely, this is a triumphant end to a long adventure.

1943. You remove the *Korowai*, the ornate woven feather cloak, I once placed around your shoulders and place it over mine.

1944. We lean towards each other to share our respective *Ha*, the Breath, the life force, together in the *Hongi*, the Intake.

1945. For the longest of times.

1946. Now, our *Whanaungatanga*—Kinship, is stronger than before.

1947. Tenei ka puawai, tenei ka whaihua.

1948. You blossom, and I am immeasurably proud of you.

1949. Neither of us utters, *Do not forget me*, but the words hang between us.

1950. I will not forget you.

1951. Until we meet again.

The Old Man leans back. Behind him, a flash of green moves at speed along the skirting. But when I look, nothing.

The Old Man, wry smile, aims a bent-finger knuckle at me—the way the old people pointed. Not intrusive, not rude, four fingers pointing back at himself. I am him. He is me.

E Moko. Kahore ano koe kia whakamarama hoki ki a ratou, he purakau ano, ne.

O, child, you haven't told them the backstory yet, have you?

About The Author

The author lives in Aotearoa (New Zealand) and hails from the northern tribe of Te Rarawa. She is a *kaitiaki*, guardian, of the once hidden writings of her great-grandfather, a *tohunga*, sage. After spending her life studying and writing about the esoteric knowledge of her people, recent world events and challenges have inspired her to share the knowledge of her ancestors. This is her first book.